The Fast-Track MBA Series

Co-published with PricewaterhouseCoopers

Consultant Editors
John Kind, Director, Human Resource Consulting,
PricewaterhouseCoopers
David Megginson, Associate Head, Sheffield Business School

THE FAST-TRACK MBA SERIES represents an innovative and refreshingly different approach to presenting core subjects in a typical MBA syllabus. The practical, action-oriented style is intended to involve the reader in self-assessment and participation.

Ideal for managers wanting to renew or develop their management capabilities, the books in the FAST-TRACK MBA SERIES rapidly give readers a sound knowledge of all aspects of business and management that will boost self-confidence and career prospects whether they have time to take an MBA or not. For those fortunate enough to take an MBA, the Series will provide a solid grounding in the subjects to be studied.

Managers and students worldwide will find this series an exciting and challenging alternative to the usual study texts and management guides.

Titles already available in this series are:

- *Strategic Management* (Robert Grant & James Craig)
- *Problem Solving and Decision Making* (Graham Wilson)
- *Accounting for Managers* (Graham Mott)
- *Human Resource Management* (Barry Cushway)
- *Macroeconomics* (Keith Wade & Frances Breedon)
- *Innovation and Creativity* (Jonne Ceserani & Peter Greatwood)
- *Leadership* (Philip Sadler)
- *Ethics in Organizations* (David J Murray)
- *Human Resource Development* (David Megginson, Jennifer Joy- Matthews & Paul Banfield)
- *Organizational Behaviour and Design*, second edition (Barry Cushway & Derek Lodge)
- *Operations Management* (Donald Waters)

The Series Editors

John Kind is a director in the human resource consulting practice of PricewaterhouseCoopers and specializes in management training. He has wide experience of designing and presenting business education programmes in various parts of the world for clients such as BAA, Bass, British Petroleum, Burmah-Castrol, DHL and Scottish Amicable Life Assurance Society. He is a visiting lecturer at Henley Management College and holds an MBA from the Manchester Business School and an honours degree in Economics from the University of Lancaster.

David Megginson is a writer and researcher on self-development and the manager as developer. He has written *A Manager's Guide to Coaching, Self-development: A Facilitator's Guide, Mentoring in Action, Human Resource Development* in the Fast-track MBA series and *The Line Manager as Developer*. He has also co-authored two major research reports – *Developing the Developers* and *Learning for Success*. He consults and researchers in blue chip companies, and public and voluntary organizations. He is chairman of the European Mentoring Centre and an elected Council member of AMED, and has been Associate Head of Sheffield Business School and a National Assessor for the National Training Awards.

Pricewaterhouse Coopers is a leading provider of professional services, including accountancy and audit, tax and management consultancy. It is the world's largest professional services practice.

OPERATIONS
MANAGEMENT

To Daphne, Frank and family

THE *FAST-TRACK* (MBA) SERIES

OPERATIONS MANAGEMENT

GALWAY COUNTY LIBRARIES

DONALD WATERS

Published in association with

PRICEWATERHOUSECOOPERS ⓡ

KOGAN
PAGE

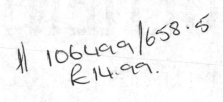

First published in 1999

Apart from any fair dealing for the purposes of research or private study, or criticism or review, as permitted under the Copyright, Designs and Patents Act, 1988, this publication may only be reproduced, stored or transmitted, in any form or by any means, with the prior permission in writing of the publishers, or in the case of reprographic reproduction in accordance with the terms and licences issued by the CLA. Enquiries concerning reproduction outside those terms should be sent to the publishers at the undermentioned address:

Kogan Page Limited
120 Pentonville Road
London N1 9JN
UK

Kogan Page Limited
163 Central Avenue, Suite 4
Dover
NH 03820
USA

The right of Donald Waters to be identified as the author of this work has been asserted by him in accordance with the Copyright, Designs and Patents Act, 1988.

British Library Cataloguing in Publication Data

A CIP record for this book is available from the British Library.

ISBN 0 7494 2776 0

Typeset by Saxon Graphics Ltd, Derby
Printed and bound in Great Britain by Biddles Ltd, Guildford and King's Lynn

Contents

Preface

Every organization makes a product. It might make tangible goods, such as cars and computers, or offer intangible services, such as education and insurance. At the heart of the organization is the set of operations that makes this product. Operations management considers the way in which these central operations are designed, planned, organized and controlled. It shows how to turn a variety of inputs into useful products.

In recent years, organizations have put much more emphasis on operations management. There are many reasons for this, including international competition, improved manufacturing processes, more emphasis on product quality, and changing customer expectations. Perhaps the most important factor has been the recognition that an organization can only be successful if it supplies the products that its customers want.

This book follows takes a logical path, through following the decisions made in an organization. The first chapter gives an overall introduction to the subject, while Chapter 2 discusses the strategic context for all other decisions. The next three chapters discuss the planning for a product, forecasting the demand, and designing a process to make the product. Once the process is in place, the organization must turn to more detailed planning, which is described in Chapters 6, 7 and 8. This planning makes the process work as effectively and efficiently as possible, and it involves a hierarchy of decisions, ranging from long-term capacity management through to short-term scheduling.

The last three chapters describe some important themes for managers. Chapter 9 looks at some ways of guaranteeing the quality of a product, and emphasizes total quality management. Chapter 10 describes some other measures of performance, such as productivity. Finally, Chapter 11 looks at the supply chain, which makes sure that there is a smooth flow of goods through the process, from initial suppliers and on to the final customers.

Taken together, the material in this book shows how managers can look at their organization's operations, and help the organization to succeed in an increasingly demanding business environment.

C D J Waters

CHAPTER I

Operations, Process and Managers

OPERATIONS MAKE PRODUCTS

All organizations make products. These products can be tangible goods – such as computers, bricks and bottles of wine – or intangible services – such as insurance, education and transport. Most products are a combination of both goods and services. At McDonalds, the product is a package that includes goods – the food you eat – and fast service; General Motors is the world's largest car manufacturer, but its products include warranties and after-sales service; British Telecom clearly gives a service, but its products also include telephones and related equipment.

At the heart of every organization are the activities that make these products. These activities are the 'operations'. Put simply, the operations describe what the organization does. Operations at IBM make computers; operations at British Airways fly passengers; at Royal & Sun Alliance they give insurance; at the BBC they make radio and television programmes; at Rosebury Junior School they educate children.

> Products are the combination of goods and services that each organization makes.
> Operations are all the activities that are directly concerned with making the products.

In principle, operations are very simple. Organizations take a variety of inputs (such as raw materials, money, people and machines), and perform operations (such as manufacturing, serving, and training) to give outputs (which include goods, services and waste material). The following are some specific examples.

- Nissan's assembly plant in Washington takes inputs of components, energy, robots, people, etc; it performs operations of pressing, welding, assembly and painting; the main outputs are cars and spare parts.

- When George Wimpey build houses, they take inputs of land, bricks, plans, equipment, etc; perform operations of brick-laying, carpentry, plastering, plumbing, etc; the outputs include houses, gardens and investments.
- The Lobster Pot Fish Restaurant takes inputs of food, chefs, kitchen, waiters, and a dining area; it performs operations of preparation, cooking and serving; outputs include meals and (hopefully) satisfied customers.
- The Open University takes inputs of students, books, buildings, staff, etc; it performs operations of teaching, research, administration and service; outputs include better-educated people, research findings and new books.

When taken together, all the operations that make a specific product form its process. The process includes all the operations for the product, from collecting the inputs through to delivering finished products to customers. The process at the *Sunday Times*, for example, starts with planning articles and sending reporters to collect stories, continues through editing, composing and printing, and on to selling papers to final customers (see Figure 1.1).

OPERATIONS MANAGERS

Operations managers are responsible for all aspects of the operations. They look after all the activities that are directly concerned with making a

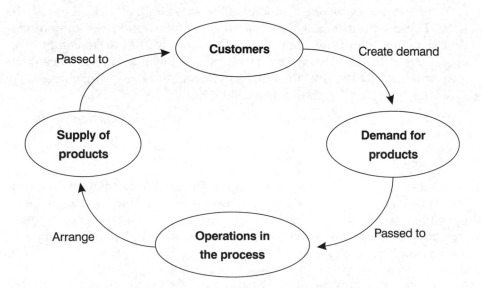

Figure 1.1 *Operations make the products that satisfy customer demand*

product – the process of collecting inputs, and converting them into delivered products that satisfy customer demand. In practice, different organizations give operations managers different titles – they are variously called 'production managers', 'account managers', 'head teachers', 'superintendents' or 'works managers'. In this book, the general title will be used, and anyone who is directly responsible for making a product will be called an operations manager.

Saying that managers are 'responsible for operations' means that their job includes the following:

- planning – to establish goals, the means of achieving these goals, and the timescale;
- organizing – structuring the organization in the best way to achieve its goals;
- staffing – making sure there are suitable people to do all jobs;
- directing – coaching and guiding employees;
- motivating – empowering and encouraging employees to do their jobs well;
- allocating – assigning resources to specific jobs;
- monitoring – to check progress towards the goals;
- controlling – to make sure the organization keeps moving towards its goals;
- informing – keeping everyone informed of progress.

These ideas are summarized in the overall view of operations management given in Figure 1.2. This shows managers making the decisions that keep an organization working effectively. Their decisions affect inputs, operations and outputs, and they use feedback about performance and other relevant information to make further decisions. Customers receive the outputs, create more demand, and give comments and opinions. The whole process works within an external environment, which includes competitors, government, national priorities and society.

DECISIONS IN OPERATIONS MANAGEMENT

At first sight, the operations in different organizations do not seem to have much in common. Operations in British Steel, for example, must surely be completely different from operations in the Crown Inn, Goldsithney. However, if you look more closely, there are surprising similarities. Managers in both organizations find the best location for their operations; they both choose suppliers and buy raw materials; they use a defined process to turn the raw materials into products; they forecast customer

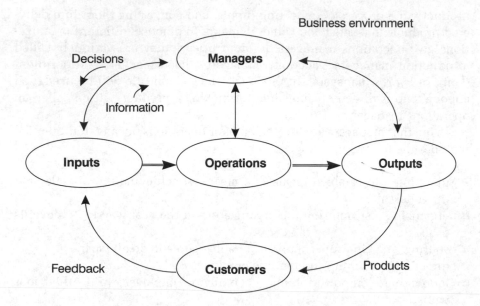

Figure 1.2 *Overall view of operations management*

demand and calculate the capacity needed to meet this; they organize resources as efficiently as possible; they are concerned with cash flows, productivity, quality and profit.

In reality, operations managers in different organizations face many common problems. The decisions needed in a Tesco supermarket, for example, will be familiar to managers in many other organizations.

These decisions in a Tesco supermarket are similar to operations management decisions in every other organization. When LG of Korea

---

Management example – Tesco plc

Tesco is the largest supermarket chain in the UK. In 1998 the company had 700 stores, 100,000 employees, 15.2 per cent of UK retail food sales, a turnover of £16 billion, and pre-tax profits of £832 million. It is continuing to expand rapidly in Britain and Eastern Europe.

The basic operations in a supermarket are quite simple. It buys large quantities of goods from suppliers, and then sells small amounts to many individual customers. However, anyone walking around a Tesco store can see many areas where operations management decisions have been made:

- Location – the location of the store must attract large numbers of customers, be convenient, have easy access, be some distance from other stores and be highly visible.
- Layout – the layout of the store, car parks and other facilities must be easy for customers to use, and must encourage them to buy goods.
- Capacity – Tesco must forecast the expected number of customers and the amounts they will buy, and then build a store with enough capacity to meet this demand.
- Product design – the product offered is a package, which includes both goods and supermarket services; this must be carefully designed to satisfy as many customers as possible.
- Process design – Tesco must design the best process for delivering their products to customers.
- Performance – performance targets are set for all operations, with procedures for measuring, monitoring and improving actual performance.
- Logistics – Tesco must develop relationships with suppliers and transport operators to get a wide range of high-quality goods delivered at the right time and at low prices.
- Stock control – the stocks of goods in the store must be big enough to meet forecast demand, but not so big that they lead to too much waste.
- Technology used – different types of technology can be used in supermarkets, including EDI links to suppliers and customers, customer-scanning of goods, automated banking, and sales via telephone or Internet.
- Staffing – the workload in a supermarket varies widely over time. Staff schedules must ensure that enough people are working at any time, but that no one is idle.
- Pricing – Tesco's policy is to offer 'guaranteed unbeatable prices', but those prices must still be high enough to make a profit.
- Vertical integration – as a major buyer of goods, Tesco could increase vertical integration by taking over suppliers.
- Maintenance – all equipment and buildings need carefully designed programmes for maintenance and replacement.
- Financing – Tesco must find the best way of raising money to finance the building and operations in their stores.

decided to invest £1.7 billion in television monitor and microchip plants in Newport, South Wales, it looked at a range of similar decisions. Graham Barnet did the same when he started a painting and decorating business in Nottingham. The most important differences between operations are:

- Volume – the total output needed from a process is usually its most obvious feature. This affects almost every decision, from the investment available to the layout of facilities.
- Variation in demand – it is much easier to run a steady process than one with widely varying demand.
- Balance between goods and services – all products are a combination of goods and services, but the balance between these puts different demands on operations.
- Variety of products – it is much easier to make standard products than a range of different ones.
- Customer contact – the amount of direct customer involvement in the process has a direct effect on the design of operations.

Whatever the type of operations, every organization must have managers who can make decisions that keep the process running smoothly. The quality of decisions made by these operations managers has a fundamental impact on the business. The right decisions can give continuing success, with customers being offered the kind of products they want. Poor decisions will give a mismatch between customer demand and the organization's products, which might be poorly designed, badly made, or too expensive. In the long term, poor operations management means that the organization is not meeting customer demand, and this will inevitably lead to failure.

This book shows how operations managers can make good decisions. It is based on the idea that organizations can only succeed by making products that satisfy customer demands. There are always competitors trying to satisfy the same demands, so operations managers must give their organization some kind of competitive advantage. They might do this by:

- making a product that no other organization can make – like Chanel perfume;
- using a process that no other organization can use – like Eurotunnel;
- improving efficiency to give a cost advantage – like National Coaches;
- increasing flexibility to customize products – like Thomas Cook holidays;
- responding quickly to changing levels of demand – like 'queuebusters' in Safeway supermarkets;

- reducing development times so that new products can be brought to the market quickly – like Toyota cars;
- scheduling operations efficiently to give short lead times and rapid delivery – like Federal Express;
- simplifying operations and making them easier for customers to use – like McDonalds restaurants;
- using convenient locations to attract customers – like Heathrow Airport;
- finding economies of scale and work at an optimal size – like Drax power station;
- designing consistent operations that guarantee high quality – like IBM computers.

OTHER IMPORTANT DECISIONS

Operations managers do not make their decisions in isolation, but work within the overall business context and co-ordinate their decisions with other functions within the organization. One traditional view is that three central functions must exist in all organizations:

- sales/marketing – identifies customer demand, stimulates new demand, collects and analyses information on customer needs, organizes advertising, takes orders and gives after-sales service;
- operations management – which is responsible for the process that actually makes the goods and services; and
- accounting/finance – raises capital, invests funds, records financial transactions, collects money, pays bills, collects cost information and maintains accounts.

These central functions are *directly* concerned with the product. There are obviously other important functions, such as human resources, research and development, information systems, administration and public relations. However, these supporting functions can either be included in one of the central functions, or are not directly concerned with the product.

Different organizations emphasize different functions. A manufacturing company might put more effort into controlling its operations, but it still needs to market its products and control its finances. A brewery might concentrate on sales and marketing, but it must still have efficient operations and control its accounts. An insurance company might focus on its financial performance, but it still has to deliver products to customers.

In practice, the boundaries between the three central functions and the various supporting functions are blurred. Procurement, for example, may be an independent support function, or part of logistics within marketing, or part of the process within operations management, or a cost centre within finance. The important thing is not to draw boundaries around such activities, but to make sure that they all work together to achieve the organization's goals. This view has led many organizations to become 'process-centred'. This means that they remove the traditional divisions within the organization, and encourage everybody to contribute directly to the process of satisfying customer demand. Separate departments, which take a short-sighted view and work on a specific task, are replaced by teams that work towards the longer aim of customer satisfaction.

A research and development department, for example, traditionally does all the technical work needed to build a prototype, and their job is finished when they pass this on to other departments. A process-centred organization has a team of people from different areas working on new product development, which becomes a part of the larger process of satisfying customer demand. R&D people do technical work for the new product, and they also become involved in other parts of the process, such as giving advice to customers.

Management example – Haflinger Electronics

Haflinger Electronics (HE) is a division of a large European conglomerate. It makes a variety of domestic electrical equipment, including radios, televisions, and CD, stereo and video equipment. In the first half of 1998 it increased its sales by 7 per cent and its profits by 10.5 per cent. This healthy performance came after many years of troubles. These started in 1972 when HE first noticed the effects of Japanese imports, and made a trading loss of £7 million. Senior managers felt that the best way to fight the competition was by improved marketing, and in the following year they tripled the advertising budget. Unfortunately, this had little success, and HE made a loss of £11 million.

The basic problem was that Japanese products were 20 per cent cheaper than equivalent ones made by HE. The company started a severe cost-cutting programme, and one of the their measures was to reduce the research and development budget by 65 per cent. Not surprisingly, HE's products soon became outdated and were overtaken by new ideas from competitors. In 1982, HE responded by restructuring. It closed down two plants, sold three others, and bought two medium-sized manufacturers in South America. In 1992, it lost £23 million, then Gareth Jones was appointed Chairman.

Jones immediately saw that, despite cosmetic changes, HE had been making the same products for 20 years, and using the same production methods. It was clear that HE could only compete by concentrating on its operations, and this meant making better products more efficiently. Jones started a 'customer focus' campaign, which found out exactly what products customers wanted. Then he invested in research and development to design products that would satisfy these demands. HE needed efficient operations to make the new products, and it built a state-of-the-art manufacturing centre in the north of England. This used just-in-time operations, and introduced continuous improvement of both products and process.

By 1997, sales had doubled, and HE was making a profit for the first time in 25 years. Gareth Jones reviewed his success by saying, 'It was very easy. We designed products that customers wanted – and then made them using the best operations. Our long-term success comes from continuous improvement to make sure our customer-oriented process stays the best in the industry.'

CHAPTER REVIEW

- All organizations make a product, which is a package of both goods and services.
- Operations are the activities that are directly concerned with making the product. They form the process that takes a variety of inputs and converts them into outputs.
- Operations managers are responsible for supplying products that satisfy customer demands. They face a range of similar problems in all organizations.
- The quality of operations management decisions affects the performance, competitiveness and long-term survival of every organization.
- Operations managers do not work in isolation, but co-ordinate their decisions with other functions, particularly marketing and finance. Many organizations are breaking down such divisions and becoming 'process-centred'.

FURTHER READING

Armisted, C and Rowland, P (1996) *Managing Business Processes*, John Wiley, Chichester

Hammer, M (1996) *Beyond Re-engineering*, Harper Collins, London

Martinich, J S (1997) *Production and Operations Management: an applied modern approach*, John Wiley & Sons, New York

Slack, N *et al* (1998) *Operations Management* (2nd edition), Pitman, London

Waters, D (1996) *Operations Management: producing goods and services*, Addison-Wesley, Harlow

CHAPTER 2

Operations Strategy

LEVELS OF DECISION

Some decisions are very important to an organization, with consequences felt over many years; other decisions are less important, with effects felt over days, or even hours.

- Strategic decisions are most important; they are long term, use many resources and are made by senior managers.
- Tactical decisions are less important; they are medium term, use fewer resources and are made by middle managers.
- Operational decisions are least important; they are short term, use few resources and are made by junior managers.

The following are some examples of these types of decision.

- For GEC, a decision to build a new factory five or ten years in the future is strategic; a decision to introduce a new product next year is tactical; a decision about the number of units to make next week is operational.
- During 1998, Royalty Trust Assurance made a strategic decision to offer single premium pensions, a tactical decision to expand the pension support office over the next year, and operational decisions about the number of staff needed in the office each week.
- Great Western Trains has made a strategic decision to continue a passenger service to Penzance, tactical decisions about the fare structures, and operational decisions about crew schedules.

The scale of decisions varies widely between organizations. A strategic decision for National Power might look at the number of new power stations needed over the next thirty years and involve costs of billions of pounds. A strategic decision for Albert Street Newsagent looks one or two years into the future, and involves costs of a few thousand pounds. The important point is that every organization has to make decisions at all three levels. Table 2.1 shows some features of the different levels.

Table 2.1 *Features of different levels of decisions*

Decision	Strategic	Tactical	Operational
Level of manager	senior	middle	junior
Importance	high	medium	low
Resources used	many	some	few
Timescale	long	medium	short
Risk	high	medium	low
Uncertainty	high	medium	low
Amount of detail	general	moderate	detailed
Data available	uncertain	some	certain
Structure	unstructured	some	structured
Manager's skills	conceptual	human	technical

Senior managers make the strategic decisions that set an organization on its course. These decisions are the beginning of a planning process that filters down through the entire organization. Strategic decisions set the context for the lower-level decisions; they pass down the organization to middle management, and give the objectives and constraints for more detailed tactical decisions. These, in turn, pass down the organization to give the objectives and constraints for the detailed operational decisions made by junior managers. The result is the familiar hierarchy of decisions shown in Figure 2.1.

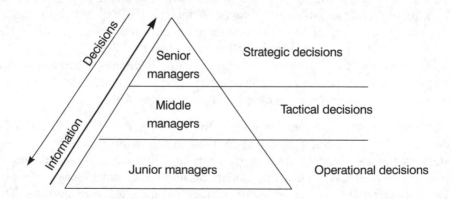

Figure 2.1 *Flow of information and decisions in an organization*

While decisions pass downwards through the management hierarchy, information about actual performance and other feedback passes upwards. This information must be filtered and summarized, or top managers will be swamped by too much detailed and irrelevant information.

Information technology is making some important changes to this traditional view. Senior managers can use improved technology to access all information in the organization, analyse it, and present it in the best format. At the same time, they are recognizing that the best person to make decisions about a process is the person most closely involved, and this is often a junior manager. The result is a squeeze on middle managers, who find that their traditional role is disappearing. Many businesses are reorganizing and downsizing, to remove layers of middle managers and to become 'flatter'. John Browne, Chief Executive of BP, has summarized this trend by saying, 'The organization must be flat, so that the top is connected to the people who actually make the money.'

STRATEGIC DECISIONS

For some people, there are really only three strategic questions:

- Where are we now?
- Where do we want to be?
- How do we get there?

In practice, strategic decisions are more complicated than this, and several different types can be described:

- mission – a statement to give the overall aims of the organization;
- corporate strategy – expands the mission to show how a diversified corporation will achieve it;
- business strategy – shows how each business within the corporation will contribute to the corporate strategy;
- competitive strategy – a narrower part of the business strategy, which shows how the business can compete effectively;
- functional strategies – which describe the strategic direction of each function, including operations, marketing and finance.

Mission

Most organizations have a mission, which is a short statement that defines their overall purpose. The mission of Halifax plc is 'to become the UK's leading provider of personal financial services'; Marks and Spencer 'aims to become the world's leading volume retailer with a global brand and global recognition'; Tarmac 'aim to be an innovative, world-class provider of high-quality products and services, which add value to our customers in the built environment'; SmithKline Beecham say that, 'health care – prevention, diagnosis, treatment and cure – is our purpose'.

Usually, the mission goes beyond a simple statement, and adds some explanations or specific goals.

Management example – mission statements

ICI

'We intend to be the world leader in the chemical industry in creating value for customers and shareholders – and to achieve it through the following means:

■ market-driven innovation in products and services;
■ winning in quality growth markets world-wide;
■ inspiring and rewarding talented people;
■ exemplary performance in safety and health;
■ responsible care for the environment;
■ the relentless pursuit of operational excellence.'

MDS Health Group

'To be a premier provider of services and products that contribute to the health and well-being of people. Our goals are:

■ *Customers*: to provide services and products which will assist physicians, health-care institutions, corporations, government agencies and communities to improve the health and well-being of the people for whom they are responsible.
■ *Leadership*: to demonstrate leadership through an ongoing responsiveness to the changing needs of clients and customers and to carry on our business in conformity with the public policy principles and goals of the jurisdictions in which we operate.
■ *People*: to maintain a climate of mutual trust which provides employee satisfaction and encourages and rewards competent, caring people to work together to achieve innovative responses to our client and customer needs.
■ *Growth*: to expand and improve the range of services and products that we offer to each of our customer groupings as well as expanding our customer and client base geographically.
■ *Profit*: to achieve a level of profitability that will provide an above average return to our shareholders, will allow us to compensate our employees justly and attract financial resources to fund our growth.'

The mission gives a focus for managers, and it makes sure that everyone is working towards the same overall goals. It also helps with a sensible allocation of resources, prevents an organization from trying to move in too many directions at once, or moving in the wrong direction, or being confused, or moving in no direction at all. Another benefit of a mission statement comes from the effort needed to get a consensus; this forces senior managers to clarify their ideas and have open debates about the organization's purpose, goals, values and identity.

Corporate and business strategy

The mission gives the context for the next set of strategic decisions. For a diversified organization, these form the corporate strategy, which shows how it will achieve the goals set out in the mission. Each business within the corporation has its own business strategy, which shows how it will contribute to the corporate strategy. These strategies typically include decisions about:

- the industries to work in;
- the level of diversification and integration;
- what type of products to make;
- organizational structure, describing the separate businesses and relations between them;
- what businesses to start, acquire, close or sell;
- relations with customers, suppliers, shareholders and other organizations;
- geographical locations for operations and markets;
- competitive position, showing how the businesses stand in relation to their competitors;
- targets for long-term profitability, productivity and other measures of performance;
- innovation, describing how the organization changes over time.

When managers design the corporate and business strategies, they have to consider three important factors: the mission, the business environment and their distinctive competence (as shown in Figure 2.2).

The business environment includes all the factors that affect an organization, but which it cannot really control, such as:

- customers – their expectations, attitudes, demographics;
- market conditions – size, location, stability;
- technology – current availability, likely developments, rate of innovation;

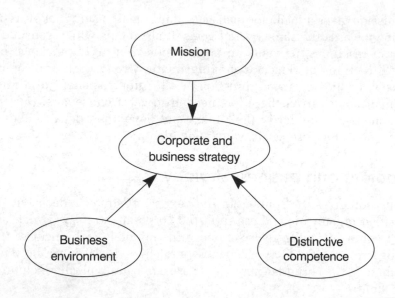

Figure 2.2 *Inputs for developing a business strategy*

- economic conditions – gross domestic product, rate of growth, inflation;
- legal restraints – trade restrictions, liability and employment laws;
- competitors – number, ease of entry to the market, their strengths;
- shareholders – target returns on investments, objectives, profit levels;
- interest groups – their objectives, how strong they are, amount of support;
- social conditions – customers' lifestyles, changing demands, significant trends;
- political conditions – stability, amount of governmental control, external relations.

The business environment is likely to be similar for all organizations making competing products, and a business can only succeed in this environment if it has a distinctive competence. This includes the factors that the organization can control, and which set it apart from its competitors. A company that can design new products very quickly will include innovation as part of its distinctive competence; other companies might base their distinctive competence on very high quality, customer loyalty, or low costs. A distinctive competence comes from the organization's assets, which include:

- customers – their demands, loyalty, relationships;
- employees – skills, expertise, loyalty;

- finances – capital, debt, cash flow;
- products – quality, reputation, innovations;
- facilities – capacity, age, value;
- technology – currently used, planned, special types;
- suppliers – reliability, service, flexibility;
- marketing – experience, reputation; and
- resources – patents, ownership.

Competitive strategy

All organizations have competitors – both the organizations that already supply similar products, and those that might start making similar products in the future. The part of business strategy that deals with competition is sometimes separated into a competitive strategy.

To develop a competitive strategy, managers must look at the organization's strengths and weaknesses in relation to those of their competitors. If a company is good at making high-quality products, while most of its competitors are producing products of lower quality, its competitive strategy could be to produce the best products available. As supermarket chains are concentrating on very large, out-of-town stores, one competitive strategy is to build small, convenient, local stores, like Spar.

The competitive strategy will only be successful if it makes products that customers want, and these products must be better than those of the competitors. Unfortunately, customers judge products using a whole range of different criteria, and it is difficult to design a product that is clearly 'better'. Some people value a brand image and buy Calvin Klein jeans; other people look at value for money and buy Eastern Butterfly jeans.

Decisions to buy a product are usually made in two stages. The first stage finds a shortlist of products that have the 'qualifying factors' – the factors that a product *must* have before a customer will even consider it. Public transport, for example, must be fast, convenient and cheap, or people will not even think of using it as an alternative to their own cars. The second stage is to look at 'order-winning' factors, in order to choose the best product from the shortlist. If several computer systems have similar specifications – they all have the qualifying factors – price and reliability might be the order-winning factors that lead to the customer's final decision on what to buy.

A competitive strategy is built around products that have all the main qualifying factors, and score well with order-winning factors. There are basically two ways of doing this – cost leadership and product differentiation:

- cost leaders make the same – or comparable – products more cheaply. They lower unit costs by having efficient operations, perhaps by improving the process, simplifying designs, reducing waste, re-engineering core functions, using higher technology, making standard products, getting economies of scale, increasing vertical integration, relocating nearer to customers, focusing on target products, or reducing the length of the supply chain;
- product differentiation makes products that customers cannot find anywhere else. There are many ways of differentiating products, based on cost, quality, performance, technology used, reliability, availability, amount of customization, delivery speed, innovation, reputation, associated services, and location.

Lyons Bakeries is a cost leader that makes standard cakes so efficiently that their unit costs are low; La Patisserie Française uses product differentiation to make different types of cakes with much higher prices. Skoda is a cost leader that makes large numbers of inexpensive cars, while Rolls Royce uses product differentiation in its competitive strategy.

It might be natural to assume that a compromise between cost leadership and product differentiation would give the benefits of both strategies. In practice, however, this does not seem to work. Companies that are stuck in the middle, making 'average' products with 'average' costs, do not perform as well as companies that concentrate on either low costs or unique products.

A successful competitive strategy is based on making better products. The products depend on the operations and process used to make them. These, in turn, depend on decisions made by operations managers. Strategic decisions of the next level are made within the functional areas. In particular, the strategic decisions that are directly concerned with operations form the operations strategy (as shown in Figure 2.3).

OPERATIONS STRATEGY

An operations strategy includes all the strategic decisions made by operations managers. It defines the overall policies for operations and gives the framework for more detailed operations management decisions.

The operations strategy forms a link between the more abstract strategic plans and the final products. While the corporate and business strategies describe general aims, the operations strategy designs the products and processes that can achieve these. Kellogg's, for example, has a business strategy that calls for market leadership in the supply of breakfast cereals, and a related operations strategy that uses large-scale production

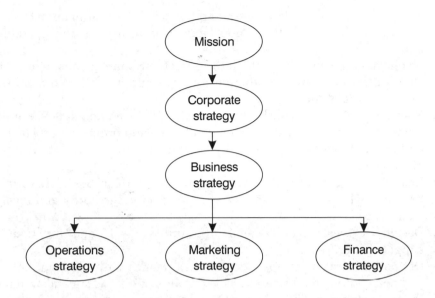

Figure 2.3 *Strategic decisions within an organization*

and distribution facilities to supply cornflakes. Southwest Airlines has a business strategy of competing aggressively on price; its operations strategy defines a no-frills, low-cost service using secondary airports, with no meals or entertainment, and a simplified booking system.

The operations strategy is really concerned with matching what the organization is good at with what the customer wants. It answers questions such as the following:

- What type of products do we make?
- How wide a range of products do we offer?
- What types of process do we use?
- What technology do we use?
- How do we maintain high quality?
- What geographical areas do we work in?
- How can we plan capacity and get economies of scale?

Designing an operations strategy

Managers can design an operations strategy in many ways. These usually involve a mixture of analysis, reasoning, experience and intuition, but there are some common themes, and a reasonable approach includes the following steps.

1. Analyse the business strategy – and other strategies – from an operations viewpoint. This gives the context and overall aims of the operations strategy.
2. Understand the market in which the operations strategy must work. This shows the kind of product that customers want, as well as the volume, range, and flexibility.
3. Find the factors that will lead to success in this market, and the importance of each one. This defines the qualifying and order-winning factors, and shows the general features that products need in order to compete effectively.
4. Describe the general features of the process that can best deliver these products. This includes factors such as capacity, flexibility and level of technology.
5. Design the best organizational structure, controls and functions to support the process.
6. Define measures to compare actual performance with planned, optimal and competitors' performance. This answers questions such as 'What do the competitors do better than us?' and 'Where are the weak spots in our performance?'
7. Continuously monitor and improve actual performance.

When designing a strategy, an operations manager does not work in isolation, but includes links to strategic decisions in related areas, particularly marketing and finance. An operations strategy of mass production, for example, must have an associated marketing strategy of mass sales, and a finance strategy of heavy investment in facilities. Unfortunately, such co-ordination always requires compromises between competing goals. Suppose that a manufacturer's business strategy aims for high profits. Operations managers might try to achieve this by reducing costs, and concentrating on a narrow range of products; at the same time, marketing managers might try to increase sales, and demand a wide range of products. There are always internal conflicts; these are best resolved by taking the decisions that best achieve the mission, corporate and business strategies.

OTHER OPERATIONS MANAGEMENT DECISIONS

The operations strategy sets the overall direction for operations within an organization. These strategic decisions lead to a series of shorter-term tactical decisions about the layout of facilities, process design, capacity planning, production planning, make/buy decisions, quality assurance, maintenance plans, recruiting, and so on. These tactical decisions, in turn,

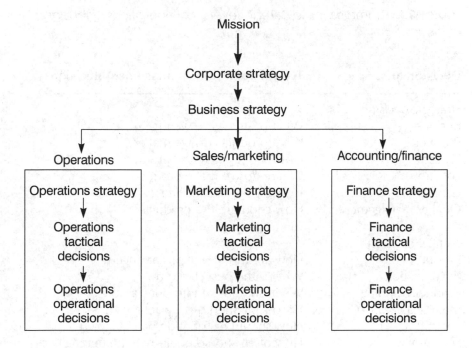

Figure 2.4 *Decisions within an organization*

lead to short-term operational decisions, including resource scheduling, inventory control, reliability, and purchasing (shown in Figure 2.4).

There is an obvious problem with the terms used here. Operations managers make decisions at all levels; it is unfortunate that low-level decisions have become known as 'operational decisions'. There are strategic decisions in operations management as well as tactical and operational ones. Table 2.2 gives some typical examples of these.

In reality, the differences between strategic, tactical and operational decisions are not as clear as Table 2.2 might suggest. Quality, for example, is a strategic issue when a company is planning its competitive strategy, a tactical issue when it chooses the best ways to measure quality, and an operational issue when testing products to make sure that they meet quality targets. Inventory is a strategic issue when deciding whether to build a warehouse for finished goods, a tactical issue when deciding how much to invest in stock, or an operational issue when deciding how much to order in a particular week.

Table 2.2 *Examples of different levels of operations management decisions*

Decision area	Typical operations management decisions
Strategic decisions	
Business	What business are we in?
Product	What products do we make?
Process	How do we make the products?
Location	Where do we make products?
Capacity	How big are the facilities?
Quality management	How good are the products?
Tactical decisions	
Layout	How are the operations arranged?
Organization	What is the best structure?
Product planning	When should we introduce a new product?
Quality assurance	How is planned quality achieved?
Logistics	How should distribution be organized?
Maintenance	How often should equipment be maintained and replaced?
Staffing	How many people do we employ and what skills do they need?
Technology	What level is most appropriate for planned production?
Make/buy	Is it better to make or buy components?
Operational decisions	
Scheduling	In what order should products be made?
Staffing	Who will do the scheduled operations?
Inventory	How do we organize the stocks?
Reliability	How can we improve equipment reliability?
Maintenance	When do we schedule maintenance periods?
Quality control	Are products reaching designed quality?
Job design	What is the best way to do operations?
Work measurement	How long will operations take?

Management example – Rover Group, Cowley

By the 1990s, a series of mergers had left British Leyland struggling as an unwieldy manufacturer trying to compete in all parts of the car market. Then, in 1994, BMW bought the remains of the renamed Rover Group from British Aerospace. Unfortunately, Rover is now too small to compete globally in the mass car market. General Motors and Ford are the largest vehicle manufacturers, with annual sales of 9 million and 7 million vehicles respectively; Renault and Suzuki rank eleventh and twelfth in size, with sales of 2 million vehicles each, and they are still four times the size of Rover.

The success of BMW has come from selling fewer cars in a more expensive, niche market. By 1998, the company had developed a corporate strategy that moved Rover in this same direction, effectively getting further away from cost leadership and towards product differentiation. The aim is to create a British version of BMW, with style, elegance and individuality that will appeal to international markets.

The corporate strategy for Rover sets the context for the business strategies of the three groups – Land Rover, Longbridge and Cowley. At Land Rover, the business strategy included a new style of off-road vehicle, and the successful Freelander was introduced in 1998. At Cowley, the business strategy meets the rising demand for luxury cars. Each business strategy leads to an operations strategy; at Cowley, this is based on the assembly of 500 luxury cars a day. The most effective way of assembling so many high-quality cars is to use a continuous assembly line, with just-in-time operations, assured quality, effective communications, improving productivity, investing in employees, and so on. The operations strategy leads to lower-level tactical and operational decisions about schedules and resources.

The overall result of these decisions is that productivity has increased from 5.62 cars per employee in 1972 to over 35, while the plant has shrunk from 104 acres to 50. Although Rover's share of the UK market has fallen to 11 per cent, it has concentrated successfully on the international market, and in 1996 exported more than half its production for the first time in its history.

Some of the decisions that operations managers make include:

- helping with the formulation of a mission, and corporate and business strategies;
- analysing these general strategies from an operational viewpoint, and defining objectives to help the organization achieve them;
- designing operations strategies for achieving these objectives;
- designing products and processes that can best achieve the operations strategies;
- managing the operations, with tactical and operational decisions to support the products and processes; and
- continually improving operations to give better performance and competitive positions.

The most important point about these decisions is that they are directly concerned with making products. Organizations need products that satisfy customer demand, and the operations managers make these. They are clearly in a unique position to affect business performance. If they make the right decisions, their organization will remain competitive and enjoy continuing success. However, if they make the wrong decisions, their organization will perform badly, and in the long term must inevitably fail.

CHAPTER REVIEW

- All organizations need decisions at strategic, tactical and operational levels. Strategic decisions are long-term, made by senior management, and involve many resources.
- There are several types of strategic decisions. These start with a mission, which gives an overall statement of an organization's beliefs and aims. The mission sets the context for all other decisions.
- The corporate and business strategies show how an organization will achieve its mission. They look at its strengths, and say how it can succeed within its environment.
- The operations strategy consists of the long-term decisions made by operations managers. It forms a link between the more abstract strategic plans, and the design of products and processes.
- An operations strategy is based on products that meet customer demands, and the process used to make these. This is a key area for decisions in every organization.
- The operations strategy sets the context for more detailed decisions at tactical and operational levels.

FURTHER READING

Baden-Fuller, C and Pitt, M (1996) *Strategic Innovation*, Routledge, London

Craig, J C and Grant, R M (1993) *Strategic Management*, Kogan Page, London

Johnson, G and Scholes, K (1997) *Exploring Corporate Strategy* (4th edition), Prentice Hall, Engleswood Cliffs, NJ

Mintzberg, H (1993) *The Rise and Fall of Strategic Planning*, The Free Press, New York

Wheelin, T L and Hunger, J D (1998) *Strategic Management and Business Policy*, Addison-Wesley Longman, Reading, MA

CHAPTER 3

Product Planning and Design

PRODUCTS AND PROCESSES

According to Michael Hammer, 'The mission of a business is to create value for its customers.' This reinforces the view that an organization can only be successful if it makes products that customers want. Chapter 2 showed how the operations strategy takes this rather vague concept of satisfying customer demand, and expands it to describe the kind of products the organization will make. The next decisions take these general ideas about kind of products, and add some details to show actual product designs. This is the basis of product planning.

■ Product planning is concerned with all decisions about the introduction of new products, changes to existing products and withdrawal of old products;
■ its aim is to make sure that an organization has a steady supply of products that customers want.

In practice, it is almost impossible to separate the design of a product from the process used to make it. The features of any product depend on its process – an airline meal made on an assembly line is different from one cooked individually by a chef. In many services, the links between the product and its process are particularly close, and it is very difficult to draw a line between the product offered by, say, the Post Office and the process used to deliver it.

None the less, an important question for some organizations is whether they have a product focus, seeing themselves as primarily making a product, or a process focus, seeing themselves as primarily using a process.

■ A company that sees itself as running a bottling plant has a process focus; one that makes bottled lemonade has a product focus.

- Expensive restaurants have a process focus – they cook foods; hamburger restaurants have a product focus – they sell hamburgers.
- A telephone company has a product focus – it arranges telephone calls; a communications company has a process focus – it enables the most appropriate communications.

This distinction may not be very clear, as all organizations both use a process and supply a product. The focus asks if the organization sees itself *primarily* as making a product or using a process. This apparently subtle difference can have an important effect on operations. If, for example, the demand for a product declines quickly, it is much easier for an organization with a process focus to adjust production; if sales of a product are stable for a very long time, it may be better to organize around the product. This chapter will concentrate on aspects of product planning, while Chapter 5 will look in more detail at the process.

PRODUCT LIFE CYCLE

The main difficulty with product planning is that customer demands change over time. In winter they want warm clothing, and then in summer they want clothes that keep them cool; ten years ago everyone wanted pine cupboards in their kitchen, but this year they want oak; they used to want portable telephones, but now they want portable Internet services. Customers change their buying habits for many reasons, ranging from fashions to new legal requirements.

As a result, the demand for any product changes continually. Sometimes, the demand follows a pattern for which there is an obvious explanation; for example, the seasonal demand for sun-tan lotion, or the peaks in demand for turkeys. Another pattern comes from the product's life cycle, which describes the overall shape of demand, from a product's introduction through to its withdrawal.

There are five stages in a standard product life cycle, as shown in Figure 3.1:

1. Introduction – a new product appears on the market and demand is low while people learn about it, try it and see if they like it. Current examples include digital versatile discs, hand-held computers and automated supermarket check-outs.
2. Growth – new customers buy the product and demand rises quickly. For example, telephone banking and genetically modified cereals.

3. Maturity – most potential customers know about the product and are buying it in steady numbers. Demand stabilizes at a constant level. For example, colour television sets and insurance services.
4. Decline – sales fall as customers start buying new, alternative products. For example, tobacco and milk deliveries.
5. Withdrawal – demand declines to the point where it is no longer worth making the product. For example, black-and-white television sets and telegrams.

The length of the life cycle varies quite widely. Each edition of a newspaper has a life cycle of a few hours; fashions in clothing and computer games have a life cycle of months or even weeks; consumer durables such as washing machines have a life cycle of several years; some basic commodities such as soap and coffee remain in the mature stage of their cycle for decades. Unfortunately, there are very few guidelines for the length of a cycle. Some products have an unexpectedly short life and disappear very quickly, while others stay at the mature stage for a very long time. Some products, such as full cream milk and beer, spent many years at the mature stage, but are now in a decline. Some products appear to decline and then grow again; cinema attendances fell from 1.64 billion in 1946 to 54 million in 1984, and then grew again to 140 million in 1997.

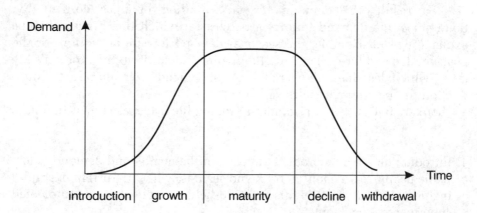

Figure 3.1 *Stages in a product life cycle*

Management example – data storage for PCs

Early personal computers did not have any secondary storage until Commodore, which dominated the market in the mid-1970s, introduced tape cassettes. These were very slow and had limited capacity. Many different formats were tested, and eventually the 5¼-inch floppy disk, holding about 64kb, became standard. In the 1980s, this was replaced by the 3½-inch 1.44Mb floppy, which is still found on most PCs.

Unfortunately, most users now find that 1.44Mb is too limiting. Photographs from a digital camera need several disks to get a reasonable picture, Windows and other standard operating systems need dozens of disks, and huge amounts of data are frequently downloaded from the Internet. At first, it seemed that the answer was to increase the capacity of the disk to create a 'superfloppy' – such as the Iomega Zip, SuperDisc and HiFD – which can hold 100–200Mb on a disk the same physical size as an ordinary floppy. However, superfloppies never really caught on, being overtaken by the now universal CD-ROMs.

The standard CD-ROM holds about 650MB of data, but initially had the disadvantage of being read-only. Now sales of CD-R and CD-RW disks are growing, but their life may be fairly brief, as they are being replaced by DVDs – digital versatile disks. Initially, 2.6 gigabyte and 5.2 gigabyte versions were introduced in 1998, with 9.4Gb versions in 1999.

Life cycles in the computer industry are short, and the end of the DVD format is already in sight. Norsam is one company using a gallium ion beam to etch data on to a nickel disk that can hold 165Gb, and this should be on the market early in the new millennium.

OPERATIONS AND THE LIFE CYCLE

The product life cycle affects operations in several ways, including the following:

■ products at different stages in their life cycle use different types of operations;
■ there are wide variations in costs, revenues and profits at each stage;
■ organizations with different expertise start – and later stop – making products at different points in the life cycle;
■ organizations usually make a range of products to smooth overall production;
■ organizations must continually develop new products to maintain their product ranges.

Different types of operations during the life cycle

Operations managers are involved with the early research and development. (For more on new product design, see later in this chapter.) When the product is launched and moves into the introduction stage, initial demand is small. This is met by small-scale operations – perhaps with individual units made for specific orders. The initial designs of the product can be adjusted as customers give their reaction, so the operations must be flexible enough to deal with changes in both demand and specifications. At the same time, they must meet due dates and quality targets so that the product gains a reputation for reliability.

If customers like the new product, the organization will increase production and move into the growth stage. The product design becomes more stable, and operations managers look for improvements in the process, typically changing from a manual process to a more automated one. The aim is to meet the growing demand, and to discourage competition by keeping quality high and unit costs low. Products are no longer made for specific orders, but are put into a stock of finished goods, from which customer demands are met with short lead times. This makes the forecasting of demand more important, with emphasis on planning and scheduling of resources. The growing demand also puts more emphasis on the supply system, which must find reliable sources of parts and materials.

Eventually, the product reaches its mature stage, when demand stabilizes; by this time, forecasting and production planning have become routine. Some early competitors may have stopped production, leaving the market to a few larger companies, who are competing on price. Operations managers now emphasize cost reduction and improved productivity, so the process may change to use more automation for standard products.

During the decline stage, suppliers will be dropping out of the market. There is likely to be excess capacity, and organizations might change the product design and the process to try to extend its life. When this is no longer worthwhile, they will design termination procedures to stop production.

Costs, revenues and profits during the life cycle

When a new product is introduced, much money has already been spent on research, development, design, planning, testing, setting up facilities, and so on. Boeing spent $8 billion in developing the B777; in October 1996, McDonnell Douglas cancelled plans to build a new MD-11, as it could not afford the development costs. Even apparently simple products can have high development costs – Cadbury spent £6 million on new production equipment for its Fuse bar in 1997, and Gillette spent £600 million before launching its Mach 3 razor in 1998. These initial development costs obviously have to be recovered from later sales.

In the early stages of the life cycle, small-scale operations mean that unit costs are high. However, the profit on each unit can also be high, as customers are willing to pay a premium for a new or novel product. The total revenue is limited by small sales, as shown in Figure 3.2.

Revenue begins to rise when the product moves from introduction to the growth stage. All being well, the fixed costs are recovered and the product starts to make an overall profit. The profit per unit can be quite high, as customers still view the product as new and are willing to pay a premium price; in addition, there is little competition, and new production equipment is working efficiently.

Revenue will rise until the product reaches the mature stage. By this time, competitors are probably making similar products and demand slackens, so both the unit price and the revenue begin to fall. Beyond the mature stage excess capacity leads to competition for the smaller demand,

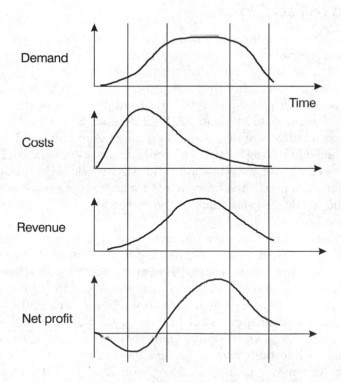

Figure 3.2 *Costs and revenues during a product life cycle*

and profits fall. Improved production methods, experience and higher productivity can offset the decline, but at some stage demand and profit fall to an unacceptable level and the organization will need to withdraw the product.

It is usually much cheaper to extend the life of an existing product than to introduce a new one. There are several ways of doing this, including:

- increasing advertising and market support;
- finding new uses for the product and, hence, new markets;
- modifying the product to make it appear new or different, by redesign or additional features;
- changing the packaging with new sizes or different emphasis;
- selling the product in new geographical areas.

The disadvantage of these changes is that they are usually short term and only really give cover until a new product is available.

Entry and exit strategies

Many pharmaceutical companies carry out basic research to develop new drugs; banks design new types of service; software houses design completely new programs. These companies look for the high profits that come from new products, but they have to bear the high costs of research and development. In pharmaceuticals, for example, SmithKline Beecham spends 21 per cent of its sales on R&D, while both Roche and Ciba have annual research budgets of over a billion pounds. According to Jean-Pierre Garnier, Chief Operating Officer of SmithKline Beecham, the key to success is 'research and development productivity'. He adds that pharmaceutical companies need three ingredients for success: research and development; the basic technologies to speed R&D; and a world-wide infrastructure to exploit discoveries.

Such companies might follow a product for its entire life cycle; for example, Polaroid invented the instant camera and has continued to make the cameras well into the maturity stage. However, most organizations do not start with basic research to develop entirely new products; nor do they continue making a product through its entire life until demand eventually dies away. Most organizations start their product planning by looking at what their competitors are making. Then they see which of the existing products will fit into their own range, and how they can modify these to create their own 'new' product. In other words, they start supplying an existing product that is already some way through its life cycle. The time when an organization starts – and later stops – making a product defines its *entry and exit strategy*.

An organization's entry and exit strategy depends on its expertise and objectives. Some organizations carry out basic research to give the ideas and technology for new developments, but they may not exploit their ideas. They work in the introduction stage and leave the market before the growth stage. Typically, such organizations are very good at innovation, but lack the resources and production skills to manage a growing demand. ARM takes this one step further. The company does the research to design high-performance RISC microprocessors, but it has no manufacturing facilities, and licenses its technology to Texas Instruments and NEC.

Other organizations look for research that has commercial potential and then exploit it during the growth stage. These aim for the high prices available during growth, and exit when profit margins begin to fall. Other organizations can design very efficient operations, so they enter the market at the mature stage and produce large quantities efficiently enough to compete with organizations already in the market. These companies exit when the product declines and the volume is too low to maintain high production levels.

These entry and exit strategies can be classified as follows:

- research-driven: good at research, design and development; innovative, with constant changes in product; high quality and high cost; low sales volumes; slow delivery;
- new-product exploiters: identifying new products with wide appeal; good at developing new processes for production; strong in marketing to create demand; high quality with reducing cost; moving to high volume;
- cost reducers: high-volume, low-cost process; low innovation, concentrating on established products; low price and fast delivery; good at process design; often automated with production or assembly lines.

Range of products made

Ideally, organizations would like to make a single product – Henry Ford famously said, 'You can have any colour of car, provided it's black'. Making a single product would give the simplest operations, with the following advantages:

- making operations routine and well practised;
- increasing employee skills, experience and knowledge of the product;
- reducing staff training time;
- allowing specialized equipment to give high productivity;
- giving long production runs that reduce equipment set-up times;
- encouraging long-term improvements to the product; and
- lowering stocks of parts and materials.

Unfortunately, the overall demand for a product usually comes from a large number of customers, each of whom wants something slightly different. Organizations allow for these differences by making a range of products – each of which is at a different stage in its life cycle – to give a smoother overall demand (see Figure 3.3).

Sometimes an organization's range of products is very wide; Thomas Cook, for example, offers thousands of different holidays. Sometimes, however, the range is very narrow; Northern Dairies concentrates on just three types of milk. Any decision about the range of products must be weighed up against the following:

- if the range is narrow, the organization can use standard operations, but some customers are lost to competitors who offer more products, or different ones;
- if the range is wide, the organization can satisfy varied customer demands, but it loses the efficiency that comes with standardization.

In effect, there is a compromise between producers, who would like to make a narrow range of products, and customers, who would like a wide range.

Organizations usually concentrate on one type of product and make variations on a basic idea. It seems obvious that a shipbuilder has the knowledge, skills and experience to build a new type of ship, but it may not have the expertise to start making perfume. Similarly, Pearl Assurance

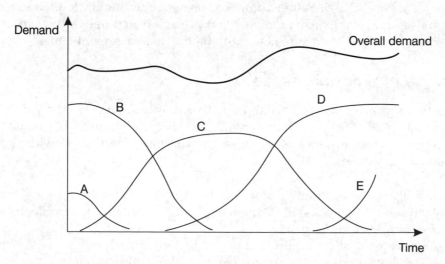

Figure 3.3 *Timing products to give a stable overall demand*

introduces new types of policy, Walls sells new flavours of ice cream, and British Airways flies to new destinations. In other words, organizations look at new products that are similar to those they already make, but are different enough to create new demands.

There are, of course, many conglomerates that make completely different types of products. Virgin, for example, has diversified into many areas, including air travel, trains, holidays, recording studios, retail shops, cinemas, a finance company, soft drinks and condoms. These areas are organized as distinct businesses, which act independently and have little contact with other parts of the group. Even so, there has been a trend away from conglomerates and towards concentration on 'core competencies'. On a large scale, companies such as Hansen, ICI and Williams have sold outlying divisions in order to concentrate on core areas (respectively, building materials, specialized chemicals, and security products). On a smaller scale, many organizations are contracting out their non-core operations; hospitals now employ catering and cleaning services, and supermarkets use specialized transport operators.

DEVELOPING NEW PRODUCTS

The product life cycle shows why older products are continually being withdrawn from the market and replaced by new ones. When the demand declines to an unacceptable level, Ford introduces a new model of car; the BBC replaces a show that has become less popular, and fashion houses replace their spring collection with an autumn one. The planning for every new product goes through a number of stages, which start with the generation of ideas and end when the product is actually sold to the customer. A common approach to this planning has six stages:

1. generation of ideas;
2. initial screening of ideas;
3. technical evaluation – initial design, development and testing;
4. commercial evaluation – market and economic analysis;
5. final product development;
6. launch of product.

Generation of Ideas

Most organizations continually search for new ideas that they can exploit. Some of these ideas come from within the organization – perhaps when a research department develops a new product. Other ideas come from outside the organization – perhaps when customers demand a product that is not currently available. Initial ideas can come from many sources, including:

- work in research and development;
- operations people suggesting changes to an existing product, perhaps to improve the process;
- marketing reports of changing customer demand;
- other internal sources;
- customers contacting the organization to suggest new products;
- focus groups organized to collect ideas from customers;
- adapting competitors' products;
- government regulations creating demand for a new product, such as sprays that contain no CFCs;
- other external sources.

People used to say, 'Build a better mousetrap and the world will beat a path to your door'. Unfortunately, the inventors of thousands of better mousetraps know that this is untrue. New ideas are easy to find; the difficult part is to look at these ideas, choose the best and turn them into viable products that customers will buy.

Initial screening of ideas

All ideas must go through an initial screening to reject those that have obvious flaws. This screening can quickly reject products that:

- are impossible to make, or are technically too difficult;
- have been tried before and were unsuccessful;
- duplicate an existing product;
- use expertise or skills that the organization does not have;
- do not fit into current operations;
- would obviously have no market;
- would obviously give no financial returns;
- are too risky.

This screening might remove 80 per cent of the original ideas (see Figure 3.4).

Technical evaluation

At this point, the initial idea seems feasible, so details are added, to take it from a general concept through to the initial designs. For this, the

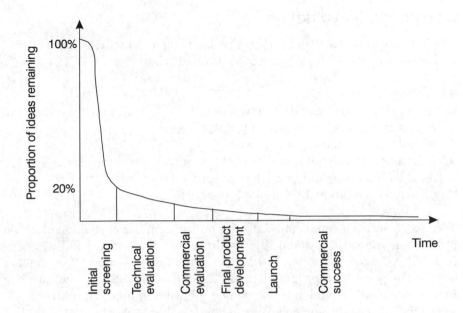

Figure 3.4 *Filtering new product ideas*

organization needs to ask two types of question: first, it must ask general questions about the concept:

- Can a product be made?
- Is the idea based on sound principles?
- Is it safe and legal?
- Is it entirely new, or a variation on old ideas?
- If it is an old idea, why has the organization not made it before?
- Are there problems with patents or competitors?
- Are developments likely to overtake the product?

Secondly, the organization needs to ask more specific questions about the product:

- Is the proposed design technically feasible?
- Can it be made with available technology?
- Does it fit into current operations?
- Does the organization have the necessary skills and experience?
- Is there enough capacity to make the product?

Prototypes and trials help with these decisions, and suggest modifications to the initial designs. The initial process designs are also considered.

Commercial evaluation

This studies the market and finances to see if the product will sell, and if it will make a profit. This stage removes products that:

- customers will not buy;
- are too similar to existing products, or are so different from existing products that customers will not accept them;
- do not fit into existing strategies;
- will not make enough profit, or have margins that are too small;
- need too much capital, or have poor return on investment;
- have too high production or operating cost.

This stage builds a commercial case for continuing the development of the product. If the case is sound, the product goes forward for full development. Unfortunately, the commercial evaluation rejects many ideas that are technically good, and people often find it difficult to accept that an idea that is technically sound may not get enough sales to make a profit.

The technical and commercial evaluation together form a feasibility study.

Final product development

Products that pass the feasibility study move on to final design and testing. This is where all the lessons learnt from previous tests – together with results from customer surveys, and any other relevant information – are used in the final designs. This stage describes the overall package that will be offered to customers, the design of any goods, the services offered, materials used, quality measures, and everything else that forms the final product specifications. This stage also finalizes the details of the process used to make the product.

Launch of product

After finalizing the product and process designs, production starts and the new product is launched. This is the first chance to see if all the planning and preparation has worked, and whether customers will actually buy the product. It would be comforting to assume that, if the groundwork has been done properly, the product will inevitably be a success, but this is not true. There are many examples of products that have been carefully planned and developed, but they still become commercial failures and are quickly withdrawn.

Some products have failed spectacularly, like the Ford Edsel, which lost $350 million in the late 1950s. In the 1970s, Joseph Schlitz Brewing Co.

made 'The Beer that Made Milwaukee Famous', but moved to an accelerated batch fermentation process that customers did not like; sales plummeted and the company never recovered. IBM's PC junior had lost $100 million by 1985. In the 1980s, Coca-Cola changed its recipe, but customers forced a return of the original 'classic' range. In 1994, Lever Brothers launched Persil Power; it was quickly withdrawn when it was found to weaken fabrics and fade colours.

Very few initial ideas – perhaps 1 or 2 per cent – complete all stages of the development process, and reach the point at which they are launched on the market. Even fewer become successful products.

Management example – Gillette Mach 3

Early in the twentieth century, men stopped using cut-throat razors for shaving, and adopted the new safety razor, which had big, disposable blades. Gillette became the world's largest supplier of these razors and blades, but, by the 1970s, they faced increasing competition from cheap alternatives. They looked for a new product, and began work on multi-blade systems. By 1976, their R&D laboratories in Reading were starting trials with two narrow blades on springs, which would follow the contours of the face and be easier to rinse. In 1989, Gillette launched this in Britain as the Sensor, with a £12 million advertising campaign. Sensor was a clear success, and was soon used by over half of all men who shaved in Britain. It had world-wide sales of 400 million razors and 8 billion blades and, as Gillette was able to charge a premium price for such a technologically advanced product, it generated more than £6 billion in sales.

Gillette continued its development of multi-bladed razors, and, in the early 1990s, developed a razor with three spring-loaded blades. They argued that this would give an even closer shave, with fewer problems for men who have never learnt to shave properly (in other words, the majority). The Mach 3 was introduced as 'the Stealth Bomber of shaving' and included 35 new features, such as 'microfins' to stretch the skin taut, a diamond-like coating on the three narrow blades, and a lubricating strip that changes colour when the blade needs changing.

The Mach 3 was launched in 1998 following a £120 million marketing campaign, and a total of £600 million in development costs. To pay for this, the price of the razor was 35 per cent higher than that of its predecessor. This was a welcome opportunity to generate higher profits for a company whose razor division had been giving disappointing financial results.

Management example – hand-held computers

Apple introduced the Newton hand-held organizer in 1992. It was never a commercial success; in common with its rivals, it was too big, underpowered, and offered no clear benefits. It was finally withdrawn from the market in 1998.

As the Newton was being withdrawn, demand for the next generation of hand-held computers was growing. The market was estimated at 3 million in 1997, and forecast to rise to 13 million by 2001. There are several reasons for this growing demand:

■ specialized machines; some hand-held computers, such as Psion's Series 5 and machines using Windows CE operating system, are small versions of desktop machines. Other machines offer specialized functions, such as Nokia's Communicator 9000 and Sharp's MC-G1, which are combinations of computers and telephones;

■ mobile workforce; employees are often geographically dispersed, but need fast, easy access to electronic communications and networks; advances in technology; the second generation of hand-held computers are much more powerful than the first generation, and much cheaper;

■ customer demand; people are becoming much more familiar with high-technology devices, and are keen to adopt new products, which can, for example, access the Internet from a hand-held machine.

CONCURRENT DEVELOPMENT

Developing a new product can take a lot of time. A new car can take five or six years to develop, Cadbury took five years to develop its Fuse bar, and a new type of insurance policy needs several years of work. The six stages described above are carried out roughly in order, but there can be much cycling and repetition. If, for example, the results of the commercial evaluation are unclear, the organization might not drop the project, but adjust the designs and return to get a new technical evaluation.

There are obvious advantages to being the first to market a new product. The first arrival will gain the price premium of new products, it can gain a dominant position, and it sets the standards for later competitors. There are also costs to consider. A longer development time ties up resources and delays the start of the income generation needed to recover sunk costs. McKinsey have suggested that bringing a product to market six months late can reduce profit by 33 per cent.

Companies that take a long time to develop new products are clearly at a disadvantage when compared with those that can react more quickly. An obvious way of reducing the development time is to use *concurrent development*. This is possible when there is no need to wait until one stage is completely finished before starting the next, so stages can overlap each other. The initial screening of ideas, for example, need not wait until all ideas have been generated; it can quickly remove obvious non-starters while other ideas are still being developed. Similarly, the commercial evaluation can be run in parallel with the technical evaluation. The more overlap that can be achieved, the shorter the overall development time – some companies have reported reductions of 30–70 per cent. Of course, this requires much more co-ordination and co-operation, and this is usually done by a cross-functional, self-directed team, which becomes responsible for the whole development process.

PRODUCT DESIGN

A common view of marketing is that an organization will be successful if it concentrates on the 'four Ps':

- product – making the right products that customers want;
- place – making sure the product is delivered properly to customers;
- promotion – telling potential customers about the product;
- price – setting a price that customers are willing to pay.

Unfortunately, many organizations fail at the first hurdle, and cannot find a product that customers want to buy. It is certainly fair to say that fewer than 1 per cent of initial ideas end up as successful products. So, what features are likely to make a product successful? A broad answer says that the whole product package must compete on cost, quality, service, reliability, availability, flexibility, delivery speed, usefulness, simplicity, location, and a number of other features. Finding a winning combination of these features calls for good product design.

People often imagine that designers are only interested in how a finished product looks, but product design is much more complicated and describes the whole product package, and the process used to make it. Burger King is not only interested in how its Whopper looks, but also how it tastes, how customers like it, how to cook it, the design of the restaurant, kitchen, staff uniforms, and all the other parts of the product package. The design must consider the entire product, which might contain:

- items supplied – goods being bought;
- environment – describes the surroundings in which customers buy;
- associated items – items that support the main product;
- items changed – customers' goods that change with the product;
- explicit services – the associated services that come with the goods and are part of the product specifications;
- implicit services – those services that are not part of the product specifications, but are still given to customers.

With a car-exhaust service, the item supplied is a new car exhaust, the environment is the workshop and waiting area, the associated items are the free coffee and other goods, the item changed is the car, which now works better, the explicit services are the guarantee that comes with the exhaust, and the implicit services include the quality of workmanship and worry-free motoring. With a restaurant meal, the item supplied is the food eaten, the environment is the restaurant, the associated items include the cutlery, there are not really any items changed, the explicit services include standards of quality and service, and the implicit services include the pleasure and prestige of eating out.

All parts of the product package have to be designed, and the design is obviously important for the product's success. Some houses sell badly simply because the rooms are poorly laid out; some VCRs do not sell because they are too complicated; some buses are not used because the times are poorly scheduled. Unfortunately, there is such a wide range of products, and so many different factors to consider, that it is very difficult to define specific features that make a good product. However, the three main requirements of a good design are that it is:

- functional;
- attractive to customers; and
- easy to make.

Functional

Functionality means that the product is able to do the job for which it is designed; it must be 'of merchantable quality and fit for the purpose intended'. This seems obvious, but there are many products – from investment services through to bottle openers – that do not work properly. As well as doing their job, products should be easy to use, efficient and reliable.

Attractive to customers

This has something to do with appearance and aesthetics, but customers judge products in a number of ways, including:

- price; if similar products are competing, the one with the lowest price will usually be the most successful. This is not always true and there are many examples, ranging from perfumes to luxury cars, where it actually seems better to charge higher prices;
- availability; a television set that you can take home when you buy it will be more successful than a similar one that is delivered in ten weeks. More people will use a bus service with regular arrivals every few minutes, than an irregular service with only two or three arrivals a day;
- quality; designed quality shows how good a product is meant to be in relation to the competition. A silk shirt, for example, has a higher designed quality than a polyester one; the Dorchester Hotel in London has a higher designed quality than Sunnyview Bed and Breakfast. A second aspect of quality describes actual achievement. Great Western Trains might suggest that a journey takes two hours, but if 70 per cent of trains take longer than this, the achieved quality is considerably lower than the designed quality;
- flexibility; a flexible company can meet specific customer demands, and react quickly to changing circumstances. This gives products that fit customer demands more closely.

Easy to make

The best products are fast, cheap and easy to make. It is fairly obvious that a product that is difficult to make will have higher costs; a product that can use an automated process will cost less than one that needs a lot of skilled, manual work. Generally, higher costs come with product designs that:

- need a lot of work in a long or complicated process;
- have steps that must be done manually;
- use non-standard procedures, parts or components;
- use too many, or too expensive materials;
- have designed quality that is too high;
- have poor achieved quality, especially if the cost of defects is high;
- have many variations or different products; or
- interfere with the production of other items.

From an operations point of view, an organization should try to simplify and standardize its product designs. Simplifying means removing unnecessary parts so that the product is easier to make. This might, for example, mean using moulded plastic parts that snap together rather than metal ones, or using a limited menu in a hamburger restaurant. Standardizing uses common components in a range of different products. This gives easier ordering of materials, discounts for larger orders, smaller stocks of parts, and longer production runs for components. Standardization does not necessarily reduce the choice available, as the standard parts can still be used in a variety of products; car manufacturers, for example, juggle standard components to produce a range of models.

Management example – Go

Air travel in Europe is dominated by a few large companies, including British Airways, Air France and Lufthansa. These airlines have traditionally given a high-quality – and expensive – service. De-regulation of the airline industry has allowed smaller companies to develop niche markets. Fairlines International, for example, offers a luxury service between Paris, Milan and Nice. A more significant development is the growth of cut-price operators.

By 1998, there were three cut-price operators in the UK: Debonair, EasyJet and Ryanair. These airlines cut costs to a minimum, by offering a basic, no-frills service. They use slightly older aircraft, secondary airports, less popular times, have a simplified booking system with no reservations, give no food or free drinks, and have fast turnarounds to increase the actual flying time of the aeroplanes. The low costs allow substantial reductions in fares, which are typically around £100 for a journey that would cost £400 with one of the major airlines. Such discount services have limited appeal to business travellers, who are more interested in convenient schedules, reliability, connections to other services and central airports. The bulk of customers using cut-price operators are leisure travellers, who are willing to put up with some inconvenience in exchange for cheap flights.

This no-frills strategy is quite risky, as the major airlines can fight competition by giving special offers, and by using the state subsidies that many still enjoy. Between 1993 and 1996, 80 new airlines were formed in the European Union, and 60 of these soon went out of business. In 1997, Debonair lost £15.4 million. However, this can still be an attractive market, with potential for rapid growth. In the US, low-cost carriers take 27 per cent of all internal passengers, and the European market is forecast to triple in size over the next four years.

In May 1998, British Airways formed its own cut-price company, called Go. This operates from Stansted and initially offered flights to Rome, Milan and Copenhagen for £100 – 20 per cent less than the three existing low-cost operators, and up to £400 less than the major airlines. In addition, the aeroplanes were newer Boeing 737s, and the flights were at peak times. Go plans to attract business travellers who are based nearer to Stansted to make up one-third of their passengers. When Go announced its new services, the existing cut-price operators complained to the European Commission that BA was using its dominant position to drive them out of business. KLM, Lufthansa, SAS, SwissAir, and Iberia all responded by cutting their costs.

CHAPTER REVIEW

- An organization can only be successful if it makes products that customers want.
- Product planning is concerned with all the decisions about an organization's products. Its aims to give organizations a continuing supply of successful products.
- Demand for all products varies over time, and normally follows a standard life cycle. This has five stages: introduction, growth, maturity, decline and withdrawal.
- As products move through their life cycle, they have different operations, costs, revenue and profit. Most organizations supply a range of related products so they can meet varied demands and maintain stable operations.
- Organizations continually update their range of products, introducing new ones and discarding old ones. There are six stages in developing new products: generating ideas, initial screening, technical evaluation, commercial evaluation, final design and launch.
- Most organizations do not develop entirely new products, but adapt existing ones. The organization's strengths and objectives determine their entry and exit strategies.
- The design of a product is important for its success. A successful design must give a product that is functional, attractive to customers and easy to make.

FURTHER READING

Baxter, M (1995) *Product Design*, Chapman and Hall, London

Cooper, R G (1993) *Winning at New Products*, Addison Wesley, Harlow

Hammer, M (1996) Beyond Re-engineering, Harper Collins, London

Hollins, B and Pugh, S (1990) *Successful Product Design*, Butterworths, London

Thomas, R J (1995) *New Product Success Stories*, John Wiley, Chichester

Wheelwright, S C and Clark, K B (1992) *Revolutionising Product Development*, Free Press, New York

CHAPTER 4

Forecasting Demand

PLANNING FOR THE PROCESS

Chapter 3 dealt with different aspects of product planning. The next step looks at the process for making the product. In particular, it looks at how organizations can organize their resources to make the product as effectively and efficiently as possible. This whole area is concerned with production planning.

'Production planning' is a very general term that describes all the planning necessary for making a product. The next chapters will look at various aspects of this planning, including the choice of type of process, capacity needed, level of technology, schedules for resources, quality management, process improvement and design of the supply system. These decisions are directly concerned with the design of the process.

There is a huge variety of processes to cater for different volumes and variations of demand, combinations of goods and services, variety of products, and levels of customer contact. The best design for the process to make any product depends on many factors, and one of the most important is the overall demand. If you want to bake a cake, it is fairly easy to design the best process for this; but if you want to bake one hundred cakes for a garden fete, you will need a different process; and if you want to bake a million cakes every week, the best process will be completely different.

All decisions about the process – and about every other aspect of planning – depend on future product demand. However, the demand for a product varies over time, and there is usually no way of knowing exactly what it will be at any point in the future. The best anyone can do is to make a forecast of the likely value. If this forecast is done well, and everything works as expected, it should provide a reasonable estimate of future demand.

Forecasts are used for all aspects of planning, and every other management decision. Decisions become effective at some point in the future, so they should be based on circumstances not as they are at present, but as they will be at the time when the decisions become effective. When British Aerospace plans its production, it does not plan enough aeroplanes to meet current demand, but enough to meet forecast demand when the planes are ready for sale. When Andy's Mobile Plumbing offers a 24-hour emergency service, it forecasts patterns of likely demand and employs enough people to cover this.

Forecasts estimate the future levels of demand for products.
Production planning sets the future levels of production, and organizes the resources needed to achieve these.

Management example – Jim Brown of Midway Construction

Jim Brown was in a bad mood. Business had been slack for the past few months, and he now had too many workers on his construction sites. He had just fired 25 people. Unless things picked up, he would have to fire another 40 people before the end of the month.

'This is crazy!', thought Jim. 'This is the sixth time in two years that I've laid off good, reliable workers. What usually happens next is that business picks up. Then I desperately look for people with the right skills whom I can hire. If I could forecast the amount of work some time in advance, I could do some planning, smooth the workload and not have to go through these peaks and troughs.'

There is one obvious problem with production planning. Operations managers like to organize the process so that it works smoothly with as few alterations and adjustments as possible (see Chapter 5), but demand for the product varies over time. The planners therefore have to find the best compromise between a variable demand and steady production. This means that they have to:

- make accurate forecasts of expected demand for products over time;
- design the best process to meet the long-term demand;
- organize resources to keep the process working efficiently;
- allow flexibility to cater for short-term variations in demand.

Another problem for planners comes from constraints on the process. If there are unlimited resources, production planning is easy. However, in reality, there are always constraints on the process; perhaps the timing is constrained, as with the *Guardian*, which must be printed and delivered to newsagents before a specified time in the morning; or there may be a constraint on cost, as with John Lewis, which is 'Never Knowingly Undersold'. In general, constraints exist on the following:

■ capacity – which gives the maximum rate at which units can be made;
■ timing – to give the times within which customers want the products;
■ cost – which limits the amount that can be spent on production; and
■ quality – describing the level of quality that customers accept.

The overall aim of production planning is to organize the resources needed to make the products; this should allow customer demand to be satisfied as effectively and efficiently as possible, without breaking any of the constraints on production.

Management example – rain and floods

The weather affects everyone, but for some people – such as fishermen, farmers and pilots – it is vital to know the weather forecast. This is why the Meteorological Office and similar organizations use the latest technology, enormous resources and huge amounts of money to make the best weather forecasts available. Despite widespread opinions to the contrary, their short-term forecasts are usually quite good, but there are still some problems.

Over the Easter weekend of 1998, eastern England saw the worst floods for 150 years. Many parts of the country were covered in snow three weeks after the official end of winter, and the exceptional weather caused damage estimated at £1.5 billion. There were some other interesting points raised by this bad weather:

■ no one had enough time to take any reasonable precautions against the floods. The amount of rain came as a surprise, as weather forecasts did not provide sufficient warning;
■ the National Rivers Authority, which manages the flow of water down many rivers, did not have enough time to implement plans for dispersing such large amounts of water. It could not prevent widespread flooding as rivers burst their banks, and there were suggestions that sluice gates were opened to deliberately flood some areas and leave other areas less badly affected;
■ Water UK said that 95 per cent of the water was wasted, and that areas under water at Easter could face water shortages and droughts in the next summer.

There are two important lessons here. First, that forecasts can always be wrong. Second, that the forecasts on their own serve no purpose; it is the way they are used in subsequent planning that is important (see Figure 4.1).

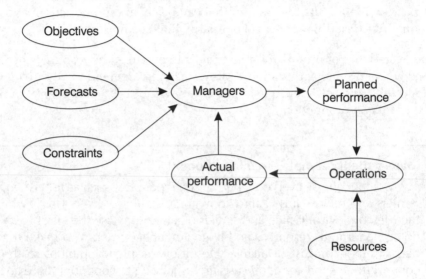

Figure 4.1 *Place of forecasting in planning*

LEVELS OF PRODUCTION PLANNING

Production planning is a part of operations management, and it needs decisions at every level – from strategic to operational. In the year 2000, the Olympic Games will be held in Sydney. The organizing committee for these games has to make long-term plans, so that it can build stadiums for all the events, accommodation for athletes, and all other facilities needed for an event that will cost several billion pounds. Medium-term plans for the months before the games make sure that all the events are scheduled, transport is arranged and other resources are properly organized. Short-term plans make sure that judges turn up to officiate at the right competitions, food is served, and all the detailed arrangements are made.

These different levels of production planning fit into the structure of decision-making already described. A typical hierarchy of production plans includes the following.

- The mission and the corporate strategy set the context for lower decisions, defining the industries worked in, and the overall direction for products.
- The business strategy outlines the general type of products made and processes used.
- The operations strategy translates the general strategic statements into long-term plans for actual products, processes and resources used.
- The operations strategy leads to tactical production plans, which give medium-term details of what products to make, and when, how and where.
- The tactical decisions lead to short-term production schedules for employees, equipment, purchases and operations.

Through all the levels of planning – from vague strategic concepts to detailed operational schedules – its objective remains the same. It aims to meet forecast demand as effectively and efficiently as possible, while keeping within production constraints. At each level, the planning is supported by forecasts covering different periods.

- Long-term forecasts look ahead several years – the time typically needed to build a new factory or to organize major resources. They look at aggregate demand, so that a hospital, for example, might forecast a total demand for 5000 patients a year. With this long-term forecast, the hospital can start planning its resources and budgets. To meet demand from 5000 patients the hospital might need a total of 50 doctors, 200 nurses, and 300 ancillary workers. It will need 250 beds and all the facilities related to these.
- Medium-term forecasts typically look ahead, more than a few months and up to about two years – this might typically be the time needed to replace an old product with a new one, or to organize less demanding resources. These forecasts look at the situation in more detail, taking the partially 'dis-aggregated' demand. The hospital might forecast 1000 emergency patients next year, 1000 surgical patients and 2500 medical patients. This might require 14 surgeons to be in post by the middle of the year, and corresponding numbers of other staff and resources.
- Short-term forecasts cover the next few weeks, describing the continuing demand for a product, and short-term schedules for resources. At this point, the forecasts cover individual products. The hospital, for example, will forecast the number of patients for each type of treatment – X-ray, heart surgery, dialysis, and so on – and schedule resources to deal with these.

Generally, long-term forecasts are concerned with strategic decisions, medium-term forecasts with tactical decisions, and short-term forecasts with operational decisions. These forecasts are done in different ways, because the time horizon covered affects the availability of historical data, how relevant this will be for the future, the time available to make the forecast, the cost involved, the seriousness of any errors, and the effort considered worthwhile.

WAYS OF FORECASTING

There are many different ways of forecasting. It would be useful to say that 'much work has been done on forecasting and the best method is . . .'. Unfortunately, this is not possible. Because there are so many different things to forecast, and so many different circumstances, there is no single method that is always best. The only sure method is to look at a variety of methods and check the circumstances in which each can be used. In general, the choice of forecasting method depends on factors such as the following:

- the time covered by the forecast;
- availability and relevance of historical data;
- type of product, particularly the balance between goods and services;
- variability of demand;
- accuracy needed and cost of errors;
- benefits expected from the forecasts; and
- amount of money and time available.

One useful classification of forecasting methods gives the difference between qualitative and quantitative approaches. If an organization is already making a product, it will have records of past demand, and will know the factors that affect this. Then it can use a quantitative method for forecasting future demand. There are two ways of doing this:

- projective methods, which look at the pattern of past demand and extend this into the future; and
- causal methods, which analyse the effects of outside influences and use these to forecast.

Both of these approaches rely on accurate, numerical data. If, on the other hand, an organization is introducing an entirely new product, there are no past demand figures which can help the organization project into the future, and it will not know which outside influences affect demand. This means that it cannot use a quantitative approach, and the only alternative is one of the qualitative methods. These are generally called 'judgemental', and rely on subjective views and opinions.

This classification of methods does not mean that each must be used in isolation. Managers should look at all available information and then make the decision they feel to be best. At the very least, every forecast should have a subjective review before it is used for any significant purpose.

Judgemental forecasting

Judgemental forecasts are based on subjective views, often the opinions of experts in the field.

Suppose a company such as Zeneca is about to market an entirely new product, or a medical team in Papworth Hospital is considering a new organ transplant, or the board of directors of BP is looking at plans for 25 years in the future. There is no relevant historical data they can use for a quantitative forecast. Sometimes there is a complete absence of data, and at other times the data are unreliable, or irrelevant to the future. As quantitative forecasts cannot be used, a judgemental method is the only alternative. Five widely used methods are:

- personal insight;
- panel consensus;
- market surveys;
- historical analogy;
- Delphi method.

Personal insight

This uses a single person who is familiar with the situation to produce a forecast based on his or her own judgement. This is the most widely used forecasting method – and one that managers should avoid. It relies entirely on one person's judgement, as well as that person's opinions, prejudices and ignorance. It can give good forecasts, but often gives very bad ones.

The major weakness of this method is its unreliability. Comparisons of forecasting methods clearly show that someone who is familiar with a situation, using experience and subjective opinions to forecast, will consistently produce worse forecasts than someone who knows nothing about the situation but who uses a more formal method.

Panel consensus

One person can easily make a mistake, but collecting together a group of people should give a consensus that is more reliable. If there is no secrecy and the people on the panel talk freely and openly, a genuine consensus can be found. On the other hand, there may be difficulties in combining the views of different people when a consensus cannot be found.

Although it is more reliable than one person's insight, panel consensus still has the major weakness that everybody, even an expert, makes mistakes. There are also problems of group-working, where 'he who shouts loudest gets his way', everyone tries to please the boss, and some people do not speak well in groups. Overall, panel consensus is an improvement on personal insight, but the results from either method should be treated with caution.

Market surveys

Sometimes, even groups of experts do not have enough knowledge to give a reasonable forecast. This happens, for example, with the launch of a new product, when it would be more useful to collect views from potential customers. Market surveys collect data from a sample of customers, analyse their views and make inferences about the population at large.

Market surveys can give useful information but they tend to be expensive and time-consuming. They are also prone to errors, as they rely on:

- a sample of customers that accurately represents the population;
- useful, unbiased questions;
- fair and honest answers;
- reliable analyses of the answers;
- valid conclusions drawn from the analyses.

Historical analogy

Chapter 3 described the life cycle of a product as having periods of introduction, growth, maturity, decline and withdrawal. If an organization is introducing a new product, it might have a similar product that was launched recently, and assume that demand for the new product will follow the same pattern. If a publisher is selling a new book, it can forecast the likely demand from the actual demand for a similar book published earlier.

Delphi method

This is the most formal of the judgemental methods and has a well-defined procedure. A number of experts are contacted by post and each is given a questionnaire to complete. The replies from these questionnaires are analysed and summaries are passed back to the experts. Each expert is then asked to reconsider their original reply in the light of the summarized replies from the others. Each reply is anonymous, to avoid undue influences of status and the pressures of face-to-face discussions. This process of modifying responses in the light of replies made by the rest of the group is usually repeated between three and six times. By this time, the range of opinions should be narrow enough to help with decisions.

Each of these judgemental methods works best in different circumstances. If a quick reply is needed, personal insight is the fastest and cheapest method. If reliable forecasts are needed, it may be worth the time and effort of organizing a market survey or Delphi method.

Projective forecasting

Projective forecasting examines historical values for demand and uses these to forecast the future. If demand for a product over the past three weeks has been 100, 110 and 120 units, it seems reasonable to suggest that demand next week will be around 130 units.

There are dozens of methods of projective forecasting. The simplest of these takes an average of past demand and uses this as a forecast for the future. If the organizer of an annual trade show at the National Exhibition Centre wants to know how many people will attend, the obvious way of estimating this is to look up records for previous years. Finding the average number attending over the past eight years, say, should give a reasonable figure for next year's attendance. This works well for stable demands, but it does not work if the demand pattern changes. If the trade show became very popular two years ago, taking the average attendance over eight years would be misleading, as the older data would swamp the later, more relevant figures.

A slightly improved method takes a moving average of the last few periods. Demand often varies over time, and only a certain amount of historical data is relevant to the future. This means that all observations older than some specified age can be ignored. Moving averages find a forecast from the average of, say, the five most recent values. Then, as a new demand is known, it is added to the average, and the oldest value is dropped.

Moving averages overcome some of the problems with actual averages, but they still have two major defects: all historical values are given the same weight; and the method only works well with steady demand.

A better approach is to use exponential smoothing, currently the most widely used forecasting method. It is based on the idea that, as data gets older, it becomes less relevant and should be given less weight. Exponential smoothing provides this declining weight by using only the latest demand figure, and the previous forecast, to calculate:

new forecast = α × latest demand + (1–α) × last forecast

where α is a smoothing constant, which usually takes a value around 0.2.

The way in which exponential smoothing adapts to changes in demand is shown by a simple example. Suppose a forecast was optimistic and suggested a value of 200 for a demand that actually turns out to be 180. Taking a value of α = 0.2, the forecast for the next period is:

new forecast = α × latest demand + (1–α) × last forecast
= 0.2 × 180 + (1– 0.2) × 200
= 196

The optimistic forecast is noted and the forecast for the next period is adjusted downwards.

These three methods are very simple, but can still give useful results. Other methods of projective forecasting are much more complicated. One standard approach assumes that the overall demand is made up by the following series of components:

- an underlying value, which is the basic demand;
- a trend, which gives the long-term direction of demand, which might be a steady upward or downward movement;
- seasonal variations, which are regular variations, typically showing how demand changes over a year;
- cyclical variations, which are longer-term variations, typically caused by business cycles.

Forecasting each component separately and combining the results gives a reasonable overall picture. However, there is no guarantee that a more complicated method of forecasting will give better results than a simple method. Sometimes a simple method will give very good results, and a very complicated method will give very poor results. There must also be a balance between the likely benefits from a forecast and the cost of obtaining it.

Whatever method is used, the calculations soon become tedious, which is why forecasting is always computerized. There are dozens of software packages available. Some of these are completely automatic, free-standing programs, which analyse a set of data, choose the best forecasting method, find the best values for parameters, and then produce the best possible forecasts. Some packages only do basic calculations and follow users' instructions blindly; some are add-ons for spreadsheets; some are parts of larger packages that integrate several functions.

Management example – generating electricity

One of the most difficult problems of forecasting is the demand for electricity. Electricity cannot be stored – except in very small quantities, using batteries – so all demand must be exactly matched by the supply from power stations.

The long-term demand for electricity is rising steadily, so enough power stations must be built to meet this long-term demand. Planning and building a major power station can take 20 years and cost billions of pounds. Smaller gas-fired stations can be built faster and more cheaply, but they are still based on forecast demand a decade or more in the future.

In the shorter term, demand for electricity follows an annual cycle, with demand generally heavier in winter, when more heating systems are switched on. There may also be short irregular periods when demand is particularly high, perhaps during very cold periods. There are also cycles during the week, with lower demand at the weekends, when businesses are not working so intensely. On top of this are cycles during the day, with lighter demand during the night when most people are asleep. Finally, there are irregular peaks during the day, often corresponding to breaks in television programmes when people turn on their electric kettles.

Power stations cannot just be turned on, but need to be prepared and warmed up before they begin to supply electricity. A relatively stable demand makes operations much easier, and electricity suppliers give off-peak discounts in an attempt to level demand. This does not really have much impact, and the suppliers still have to forecast demands with a long-term trend, annual cycle, periods with changes, weekly cycles, daily cycles and short-term fluctuations. Then they have to plan the electricity supply to meet this ever-changing demand from the cheapest possible sources.

Causal forecasting

Causal forecasting uses a cause-and-effect, or other relationship, between variables to forecast unknown values.

The likely number of reports written by a management consulting firm next year could be calculated by looking at the number of reports written in past years, and projecting this pattern into the future. However, the number of reports will probably depend directly on the number of people employed. It might be possible to get a much more reliable forecast for the number of reports by looking at the number of people the firm plans to employ next year. This kind of relationship – between the number of reports and the number of people employed – is the basis of causal forecasting.

This kind of relationship is encountered all the time. The sales of a product depend on the price, so the proposed price may be used to forecast likely sales; the output from a machine depends on the speed it is set to work; productivity depends on bonus payments; the amount of money borrowed depends on interest rates; crop size depends on the amount of fertilizer used. By setting the value of one of the variables, it is possible to forecast the value of the other.

Linear regression illustrates the approach of causal forecasting. This assumes that there is a linear relationship between two variables. Suppose, for example, that an organization has plotted the output from a process against the corresponding number of shifts worked, as shown in Figure 4.2. A trend line can be fitted through the points to show the underlying pattern. From this it is possible to see that a factory that works 50 shifts next month can forecast output as around 400 units. As with projective forecasting, the calculations for regression are always done by computer.

ERRORS IN FORECASTS

The problem with forecasts is that they are usually wrong. If the Government forecasts inflation next year at 2.2 per cent, it is likely to be somewhere around there – perhaps 2.6 per cent – but it is unlikely to be exactly 2.2 per cent. Similarly, if we forecast sales of 2,000 units next month, we will hopefully be somewhere close, but will not be surprised if there is an error. If the actual sales turn out to be 1,900, we will be quite pleased that the forecast was so good, and if actual sales are 900 we will be rather disappointed to have such a big error. We would certainly be surprised if sales turned out to be exactly 2000 units.

The reason for this is that demand always contains a random element that cannot be foreseen. Customer demand varies continually. Some of this variation can be explained by seasonal variations, trends, or the effects of a life cycle, but, even if the patterns are analysed as carefully as possible, there are some effects that cannot be explained. These are the 'noise' – the random elements that cannot be forecast. The 'noise' is the reason why it

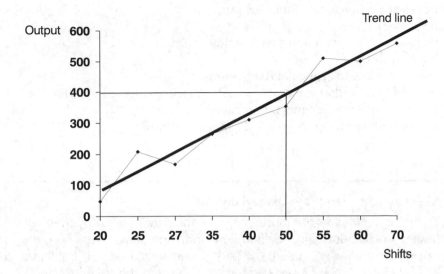

Figure 4.2 *An example of causal forecasting*

sometimes takes 22 minutes to drive to the next town, and sometimes 19 minutes; it is the reason why it is not possible to predict reliably the price of shares or gold, how long it will take to paint a room, or even which team will win a football match.

Because of the noise, forecasts are always likely to contain errors. The effects of this noise can be minimized by using a suitable forecasting method, choosing the best parameters, looking at aggregate demand rather than individual demands, and making short-term forecasts rather than long-term ones. However, it is not possible to eliminate the effects completely. This does not mean that the forecasts are of no use. If the forecasts are done properly, and the amount of noise is reasonably small, the errors should be within acceptable limits. Serious problems really only arise if there is some fundamental mistake in the forecasting, or if there is too much noise.

Remember that, however big or small the errors are, forecasts still give the best estimates of future values. The only alternative to using forecasts is to make decisions without using any information at all, and this would certainly be disastrous.

A good forecast's errors must be small, but there are several other requirements. It must:

- forecast the demand really needed – and not a similar demand that is easier to find;

- be ready in time for its intended purpose;
- be cost-effective;
- be in a useful format and easy to understand;
- have small errors;
- give an idea of the range of likely errors;
- be unbiased, so that forecasts are not consistently too high or too low;
- be responsive to changing circumstances;
- be not unduly affected by the odd unusual result.

Management example – Disneyland Paris

Disneyland Paris was the fourth major theme park opened by the Walt Disney Corporation, after California, Florida and Tokyo. However, for several years after it opened, the park had serious financial problems, and by March 1994 it faced permanent closure. At this time its owners – 61 banks and other investors – agreed a rescue package valued at Fr 13 billion.

The basic problem was that the income of Disneyland Paris was not meeting its costs. The capacity of the park, the number of people employed, the number of rides, and almost every other aspect of operations were based on forecasts of the number of visitors. There were no other Disney parks in Europe, so these forecasts were based largely on American experiences. Unfortunately, later results showed that there were significant differences in Europe.

In 1993, the park attracted nearly 10 million visitors. Despite the considerable effort put into forecasting, this was 13 per cent fewer than expected. At the same time, each visitor spent at least 10 per cent less than forecast. The result was an annual loss of Fr 5.34 billion, which grew worse when 1994 saw fewer than 9 million visitors.

All decisions about Disneyland Paris had, therefore, been based on faulty forecasts. When actual performance became known, the theme park had to make significant changes to operations. They tried to attract more visitors, by cutting prices, reducing hotel costs, introducing seasonal pricing in the autumn and winter when only 30 per cent of visitors came, special deals for pensioners, school groups and 'kids-free' packages, placing more emphasis on short packages, and carrying out more promotion in Britain. Several other measures were agreed with the Walt Disney Corporation, which owns 49 per cent of the park. These include Fr 1.1 billion of extra credit, selling Fr 1.4 billion of assets to Disney and leasing them back at favourable terms, the waiving of royalties on entry fees, food and merchandise, and suspending management fees. Other plans included greater cost control, a new shopping mall, a multiplex cinema, new restaurants, more convention facilities, a high-speed rail link and improved access. These measures were aimed at making the park financially secure by 1997.

Management example – McGraw, Finch and Happendon

Colin Fairweather has retired as Senior Partner in the Management Consultancy firm of McGraw, Finch and Happendon. Before he left, he collected some ideas in a series of notes for his future replacements. A lot of his work involved forecasting, and he wrote the following guidelines on this subject.

How to do a forecast:
1. Clearly define the purpose of the forecast. This should say what you are trying to forecast, why, how you will use the forecast, when you will need the forecast, and how detailed it should be.
   Say what time horizon the forecast must cover – perhaps forecasting demand for the next six months or two years.
2. Choose a suitable forecasting method, preferably quantitative. This choice will depend on many things, but the availability of historical data is one of the most important.
3. Collect any historical data needed for your model, and test both the data and the model.

Implement the forecasts and track their performance over time by comparing the forecast with actual demand. If the errors are too large, change the method or parameters used.

What goes wrong with forecasts:
- Forecasters do not involve other people. Remember that a good forecast is not just playing with numbers, but depends on many internal and external factors. It is always best to involve knowledgeable people in the forecasting process.
- People can have too high expectations of a forecast. Warn them about possible errors, so they will not be disillusioned if the forecast turns out to be wrong.
- Forecasts often give too much detail. This typically happens when demand is forecast for individual items, when it would make more sense to forecast for groups of items.

- Always recognize different people's needs. Sales people, for example, often like forecasts to be optimistic, while finance people prefer a more pessimistic view.

CHAPTER REVIEW

- Production planning is a general term for decisions about the way a product is made. It sets the future levels of production, and organizes the resources needed to achieve these.
- Production planning takes place at every level in an organization, and is based on corresponding forecasts.
- All plans – and every other decision within an organization – depend on forecasts of future demand. These forecasts cover varying periods, for the long, medium and short terms.
- There are many different ways of forecasting, each of which is best in different circumstances. Three basic approaches are judgemental, projective and causal.
- When there is no relevant quantitative data, judgemental or qualitative methods must be used. These are based on opinions from experts – and range from personal insight to the more formal Delphi method.
- Projective forecasts look at the patterns in historical data and project these into the future.
- Causal forecasts use relationships between variables to estimate future values.
- All forecasts contain errors, which are caused by the unpredictable noise. Although this noise cannot be eliminated, its effects should be made as small as possible.

FURTHER READING

De Lurgio, S A (1998) *Forecasting Principles and Applications*, Irwin-McGraw Hill, New York

Ellis, D and Nathan, J (1990) *A Managerial Guide to Forecasting*, Graceway Publishing Co., Flushing, New York

Hanke, J E and Reitsch, A G (1989) *Business Forecasting* (3rd edition), Allyn and Bacon, Boston

Wheelwright, S C and Makridakis (1989) *Forecasting Models for Management* (5th edition), John Wiley, New York

CHAPTER 5

Designing the Process

PROCESS PLANNING

Chapter 4 introduced the idea of production planning, which organizes the resources needed to make a product. The next few chapters will look at different aspects of this planning. We start here by asking some general questions about the design of the process.

Most products can be made by a number of different processes. A table, for example, can be hand-built by craftsmen; it can be assembled from bought-in parts by semi-skilled people; it can be made automatically by machines on an assembly line; or it can be moulded in one piece from plastic. Each process gives a product with different characteristics. So operations managers have to design a process that will make a product with the features described in the product plans. This is the function of process planning.

- The process describes the operations used to make a product.
- Process planning makes the decisions about a process. It designs a process that will make a product as effectively and efficiently as possible.

Customers are primarily interested in the product they buy, rather than the process used to make it. However, it is not really possible to separate the two, as the product inevitably depends on the process. With services, the links between product and process are very close, and it is difficult to draw a line between the product offered by a bank, theatre or taxi service, and the process used to deliver it. This close connection shows why it is so important to plan the process:

- the object of all organizations is to make a product that satisfies customer demand;
- the product must, in some way, be better than competitors' products;
- the process makes the product;
- to make better products an organization needs a better process.

PROCESS-CENTRED ORGANIZATIONS

Many organizations place such emphasis on the process that they have become process-centred. They argue that even the best product available will soon be overtaken by improved technology, competitors' designs, or changing demands. They prefer, therefore, to concentrate not on the short term and on current product designs, but on the longer term and on the process that can deliver a stream of products for the future. Pfizer, for example, makes the hugely popular, and currently unique drug Viagra. A process-centred organization would argue that this will inevitably be overtaken by competitors, and that Pfizer should concentrate not on Viagra, but on the process used to develop it, and similar drugs, in the future.

A process-centred organization looks at the whole process of satisfying customer demand. This is the reverse of specialization, which divides the process into a number of tasks, each of which is largely self-contained. When an order comes to a traditional organization, everyone works on their separate part of the process – manufacturing makes the goods, warehousing adjusts the stocks, transport delivers the goods, accounting sends out the invoices. Each of these parts essentially works in isolation. Inventory controllers, for example, do a good job if they reduce the investment in stocks and still give a good average service, but they are not directly concerned with making sure that a particular customer receives an order. Similarly, the job of salespeople finishes when a customer has collected an order, and the job of a manufacturing department ends when it has passed products to the stock of finished goods. The problem is that no one looks after the whole process, or integrates the different operations, or even makes sure that the customer actually gets the products.

In a process-centred organization, inventory control becomes a part of the supply chain, with the purpose not of minimizing costs, but of helping to satisfy customer demands. In the same way, every other job is judged by its contribution to the satisfaction of customer demand. This emphasis on customers leads to an interesting change of attitude. For many years, it was accepted that operations would be smoothest when customers were kept at a distance. The belief was that, if customers became involved, they would try to expedite their own order, change designs, demand adjustments to the products that were difficult, ask for detailed progress reports, and generally interrupt the smooth flow of operations. The best way of preventing this was to keep customers at a distance from the process. However, it would be strange for a process-centred organization, whose aim is only to satisfy customers, deliberately to keep them at a distance. The alternative is to welcome direct customer involvement, and to form a partnership in order to increase satisfaction with products, and to give an overall competitive advantage.

In a process-centred organization, everyone works as a team, with:

- the single purpose of satisfying customer demand;
- concentration on the whole process of delivering products that customers want;
- expansion of traditional roles; empowered employees make decisions and deal with all types of customer issues;
- access to all types of information throughout the organization;
- a matrix or cross-functional management structure.

As a result, when customers approach the organization, they have what Jan Carlzon, former chief executive of Scandinavian Airline Systems, describes as a 'moment of truth'. This is the point when they meet an empowered employee who can act for the entire organization. Customers effectively see a single face from the organization, the face of one person who can deal effectively with their questions, and is not passed from one area to another.

This team of empowered employees is managed by a single operations manager – sometimes called the 'process owner' or 'case manager' – who is responsible for the design, development and smooth working of the process. To design the process, this manager has to ask questions such as the following:

- What should the process really give to customers?
- How much flexibility do they want?
- How much will they pay for the products?
- What is the best type of process?
- How much automation should be used?
- What is the best layout for operations?

The answers to such questions will set the overall features of the process.

PROCESS DESIGN

The process should be designed to deliver the products in the best possible way. The customers of a football team (the crowd) want to watch exciting matches, at convenient times and in convenient locations, and to enjoy good public transport to the ground, comfortable seats, reasonable prices,

Management example – opticians as retailers

There are about 3,000 opticians' shops in Britain supplying prescription glasses. Their service has traditionally been broken into a series of distinct tasks. One group of people organizes eye tests and gives information, another group actually tests eyes and prescribes lenses, another group makes the lenses, another designs frames, another sells frames to customers, and another group treats eye disease.

However, the industry has been affected by major changes:

- chains of opticians are taking a larger share of the market, led by Dolland and Aitchison, Specsaver, Boots Opticians and Vision Express;
- sales are continuing to rise, due to an ageing population, and eyewear being worn as a fashion accessory;
- more regular and rigorous eye tests, developments in contact lenses, and non-essential uses such as driving;
- deregulation of the sale of spectacles in 1986 has encouraged non-traditional suppliers, led by Asda and Tesco supermarkets;
- there is more sophisticated equipment for automatic testing and monitoring of eyes.

Partly as a result of these changes, too many companies were competing for business and the number of opticians' shops started to decline. The biggest chain, Dolland and Aitchison, fell from 500 shops in 1992 to 427 in 1998. Increased competition encouraged opticians to become more process centred, and look at the overall process of satisfying customer needs. This led to many changes, with opticians moving away from their professional roots and emphasizing their work as retailers. They stopped looking at the industry as a series of distinct operations, and looked at the overall process of supplying glasses to customers. This means that they now pay more attention to customer service and quality; they stock more frames in the shops; 'in-store glazing' makes lenses in the shop so that finished spectacles are supplied during a single visit; some costs have declined with new testing equipment and procedures; computer simulations show the effects of different frames; and there are closer links between opticians, ophthalmologists and other medical services.

and high quality associated goods. The process should be designed to give all of these as efficiently as possible. While it is not possible to describe how to make every product, it is useful to make some general suggestions, starting with a description of the types of process available.

Types of process

The best way of classifying processes is by the frequency with which products change. At one extreme are continuous flows, like an oil refinery or electricity supply, which make the same product without any changes for 24 hours a day. At the other extreme are projects that make a single unique product, like building the Channel Tunnel or writing a book.

The types of process are as follows:

- project;
- job shop;
- batch;
- mass production;
- continuous flow.

These terms sound as if they refer to manufacturers. This may be a clue to their origin, but the principles now apply to every kind of organization, as can be seen from the examples that follow. Some people try to use completely different terms for services, referring, for example, to 'mass service' rather than 'mass production', but this becomes rather confusing. As always, we will use the term 'product' to describe the whole package of goods and services that an organization makes, and use the same names to describe processes in any type of organization.

Project

This process makes a single unit, usually tailored to individual customer specifications. Building a Formula 1 racing car, designing an investment portfolio and building the rail link to the Channel Tunnel are projects.

Each project makes a product that is essentially unique, so the process sees much variety, with little standardization. The process must have the flexibility to deal with new situations and problems, and this needs a skilled and well-trained workforce that is capable of using general-purpose equipment. Although the number of units made is low, each can involve a significant amount of work. This kind of process usually has very high unit costs. It is also the type of process with which people prefer to work, as there is more variety, the work is interesting, and they get satisfaction from contributing to an identifiable end result.

Examples of projects are the development of software for a new computer system, preparing a management consultant's report, writing a book, ship-building and building an office block.

Job shop

This makes small numbers of a wide variety of products. It gets its name from small engineering works that make products to customer specifications. For example, if the MG Owners Club wants some special sets of chromium wheel trims, they will probably be made in a job shop.

Job shops make a narrower range of products than projects, but there is still a lot of variety. The process uses general-purpose equipment, which must be set up and changed every time a new product is started. Each product goes through a different sequence of operations on the equipment. This needs flexibility from equipment and a skilled workforce.

Each product will use only some of the resources available, which means that many of the resources are idle at any one time. This will be either because of short-term mismatches between capacity and workload, or because of the set-ups between different jobs. The average utilization of resources is low – typically 25 per cent, and often as low as 5 per cent or 10 per cent – but at other times there are bottlenecks as some resources are temporarily overloaded. The result is that job shops have low capital costs, but high unit costs. The mix of different products makes scheduling and keeping track of work difficult.

Examples of job shops are restaurants, travel agents arranging holidays, makers of specialized vehicles, printers, and furniture manufacturers.

Batch processing

This makes larger batches of similar products on the same equipment. Every time a new product is started there are set-up costs, and these can be reduced by making more units in each run. Over time, a series of batches are made, with goods held in stock until they are needed to meet customer demand.

This process is useful for medium volumes of products, with less product variety and customizing. Equipment is still fairly general, but there is room for some specialization. The process has less frequent set-ups and changes, but some skilled workers are still needed.

Examples of batch processing are book publishing, insurance companies processing different types of policies, pharmaceuticals and clothing manufacturers and bottling plants.

Mass production

This is typical of an assembly or production line that makes large numbers of a single product. Computers, cars and washing machines are made using mass production. There is very little variety in the product, except small changes to the basic model, which are introduced in the finishing.

Mass production processes use specialized equipment to meet a steady, high demand for a product. As the product does not change, there are no disruptions to the process and few management problems. There is, for example, no need to schedule individual pieces of equipment or check the progress of individual units of the product. Once the process has been set up, it needs a small workforce to keep it functioning and, in extreme cases, may be completely automated. Unit costs for mass production are low.

Examples of mass production are the processing of photographs, newspaper printing, and the manufacture of cars, computers, consumer electronics and domestic appliances.

Continuous flow

These are used for high volumes of a single product or small group of related products, such as bulk chemicals, oil and paper. The process is different from that of an assembly line, as the product emerges as a continuous flow rather than discrete units. Such processes use highly specialized equipment that can work for 24 hours a day with virtually no changes or interruptions. The process is capital-intensive, but it needs a very small workforce and thc high volume leads to low unit costs.

Examples of organizations using continuous flow are petrol refineries, breweries, paper mills, sugar refineries, and the police service.

		Volume				
		Very low	Low	Medium	Very high	Continuous
	None	None – unit costs are too high				Continuous flow
	Little				Mass production	
Product variation	Medium			Batch		
	High		Job shop			
	Very high	Project				None – capital costs are too high

Figure 5.1 *Types of process and their product variation and quantities*

Table 5.1 *Features of different types of process*

Process type	Project	Job shop	Batch	Mass production	Continuous flow
Volume	one	low	medium	very high	continuous
Product variation	one-off	high	some	little	none
Product changes	n/a	frequent	some	none	none
Equipment	general	general	some specialized	specialized	very specialized
Employee numbers	many	many	medium	few	few
Skill level	high	high	medium	low	low
Capital cost	low	low	medium	high	very high
Unit cost	high	high	medium	low	low

These different process types can be illustrated by looking at the services given by restaurants. Some specialized restaurants allow customers to phone their orders in advance and the restaurant prepares the meal they request; this is a project. Expensive restaurants have a specialized menu and the preparation of any meal is like a job shop. Canteens and cafeterias have set meals, which they make in batches. Busy hamburger restaurants work in the same way as mass production assembly lines. A meal is a discrete product, so it is difficult to describe a continuous flow process, but coffee or beer served with a meal approaches this. The types of process are suited to different production quantities and variety of products, as shown in Figure 5.1. Some other important differences between the types of process are suggested in Table 5.1.

Choosing the best type of process

The best type of process depends on many factors, primarily the overall demand. Sometimes, this can be linked to the stages in a product's life cycle. During the development stage, small numbers of prototypes may be made as projects. During the introduction stage, demand is small and several variations may be used to test market reaction; these are best made by a job shop. As the product moves through introduction and into a growth stage, the variety of products is reduced and batch processing is the most effective. As the product moves to maturity, demand is stable, product variation is reduced further and mass production is best.

Management example – Henry Penhaligan Watercolours

Henry Penhaligan lives in St Ives, Cornwall. Twenty years ago he began to paint watercolours of the local coastline. These sold well to tourists, but he found it difficult to make a comfortable living. His alternatives for increasing his income were to charge higher prices, or to paint more pictures. He ruled out the first option, because tourists would not pay much more than his current prices, and decided to paint more pictures. Henry realized that the best way to increase his output was to change the process he was using. Originally, he had used a project process, in which each picture was a unique product. Although it meant a fundamental change to his products, he decided to aim for higher sales of mass-produced pictures. This meant making standard products – typically, a view of the coast with cliffs and a beach – and having different people work quickly on each painting. One person would paint the sky and cloud formations, a second would add the cliffs, a third would paint the sea, a fourth would add the beach in the foreground, and so on. This was equivalent to a job shop process.

Eventually, Henry refined the process so it became almost a mass production. Paintings moved past a series of artists, with each of them adding a small part to the picture. Using this method, a painting could be finished in under an hour. The final product is obviously very different from the original paintings, but the output has risen dramatically.

This is, of course, an idealized picture, but it shows how an organization needs to make continual adjustments to both the product and process as they move through the product's life cycle. Most of the changes in the product occur earlier in its life cycle, and the designs become more stable over time. With the process, there is more innovation later in the life cycle, as shown in Figure 5.2.

There are many factors to consider before choosing the type of process, including the following.

- Product design; to a large extent, the product's design will set the best overall type of process. When Giuliano Marotti designs a very high-quality suit to specifications given by a customer, the process is fixed as a hand-made project rather than mass production. Most good designs allow different types of processes, or at least significant variations on a single type.
- Overall demand; the number of units made clearly affects the best type of process. Portraits, for example, can either be painted or photographed

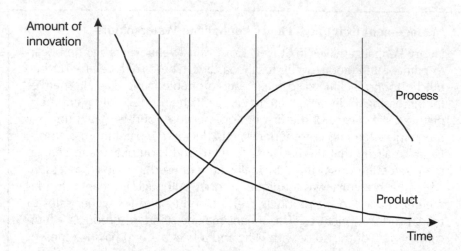

Figure 5.2 *Amount of innovation during a product life cycle*

– painters use a project process to make very small numbers, while film processors use mass production for very large numbers. Higher demands allow an organization to use lower-cost processes.

■ Changes in demand; if the number of units made has to change continually to meet a variable demand, a more flexible process must be used. This must have enough capacity to meet peak demands, but still work efficiently during slacker times. Hotels, for example, must cater for large numbers of guests in holiday seasons, but still work efficiently with smaller numbers out of season.

■ Product flexibility; this shows how quickly a process can stop making one product and start making another. Generally, the lower-volume processes are more flexible to changes in both demand and product.

■ Human resources; different processes need different skills in the workforce – and the availability of workforce skills, management skills, training and productivity targets affect the choice of process.

■ Automation; higher levels of automation are generally associated with expensive, specialized equipment making high volumes, so the level of automation used by the organization can affect its choice of process. In practice, this traditional view is changing, and flexible automation can make small numbers of products very efficiently.

■ Customer involvement; customers are not usually involved in manufacturing, but they can play an active part in services, as in self-service petrol stations, buffets in restaurants, and automated banking machines. More personal services generally need processes that allow higher customer involvement.

- Product quality; the traditional means of getting high quality was to use highly skilled craftsmen to make small numbers of a product. These craft processes are still best for some products, but automated processes give high quality for a wide range of other products. The most reliable computers, for example, are not hand-made, but come from automated assembly lines.
- Finances; the costs of setting up different processes vary widely, so the choice can be affected by the capital available and installation cost. In turn, the process chosen affects the operating expenses, return on investment and purchase price of the product.
- Amount of vertical integration; vertical integration refers to the amount of the supply chain that is owned by one organization. When a process considers the whole mechanism for delivering products to customers, it might make sense to have more of this under the control of a single organization. There is usually more vertical integration with higher-volume processes.

PROCESS TECHNOLOGIES

Different types of process generally use different levels of technology, with higher production using higher levels of technology. This technology can be described as:

- manual;
- mechanized; or
- automated.

A manual system has one person with full control over the process, which needs their continuous attention. Driving a bus is an example of a manual process.

A mechanized system needs people for parts of the process, but once started, it can work to some extent without further intervention. Using a VCR is an example of a mechanized process.

Automated systems can work without any human involvement. A telephone exchange uses an automated process.

A manual warehouse has people physically putting goods on to shelves and later removing them for customers; a mechanized warehouse has people using stacker cranes; an automated warehouse has a computer that automatically controls all stock movements. A manual system for sorting letters has people putting letters into appropriate bags; a mechanized system has a person who reads addresses and directs equipment to move letters; an automated system has scanners to read the post code and automatically route letters.

As higher levels of automation are generally used for higher volumes of output, it is possible to say that:

- projects and jobs shops usually have manual processes;
- batches have mechanized processes;
- mass production and continuous flows use automation.

AUTOMATION IN SERVICES

The term 'automation' might conjure up an image of robots working on a production line, but in recent years much more effort has gone into automating services. Many services – such as those offered by dentists, lawyers, doctors, accountants, hairdressers and taxis – are produced either singly or in very small batches. Each customer demands a different product from the service, so it uses a project or job shop process. This inevitably gives higher costs. However, many services – particularly the routine ones that offer a standard product – can use a lot of automation. This might automatically process customers themselves (such as ChampionChips, which record runners' progress in a marathon), customers' materials (such as baggage-handling equipment in an airport), information (such as Shell customer reward cards), or create new services (such as Internet shopping). The following examples illustrate automation in services.

- Offices – clerical jobs have been transformed by technology, as computers have taken over almost all the traditional jobs of preparing, storing, analysing, copying and transmitting documents and information.
- Banks – almost all transactions in banks are automated, using a combination of magnetically coded plastic cards, optical character readers, and cash-dispensing machines.
- Supermarkets – most supermarkets use a mechanized system, in which checkout operators add the costs and present a bill. There are several alternatives for automated systems, including self-scanning, computer-readable shopping lists, virtual shopping via the Internet, telephone shopping and automatic delivery systems.
- Post Office – sorting letters has become largely automated with the use of post codes, but the need to send letters has also been reduced by computer networks, e-mail and fax machines. In 1993, the number of letters posted declined for the first time.
- Warehousing – some warehouses are now completely automated, with computers recording all stock movements and controlling the physical handling of goods.

- Reservation systems – airlines started using on-line reservation systems in the 1960s. They are now essential for smooth operations, and are used for many other activities, including buses, trains, theatres, concerts and sporting events.

Management example – automatic banking machines

Banks have used automation for many years. Their internal administration is largely computerized, and they encourage customers to withdraw cash from simple cash-dispensing machines. More advanced machines allow customers to pay bills, transfer funds, update account information, use credit cards, and carry out most of their usual banking tasks. Such automated banking machines have obviously reduced the amount of personal service, but they also give lower costs, less paperwork and fewer mistakes.

The next generation of machines allows some contact with bank staff. All the main banks have experimented with virtual branches, which can be little more than kiosks in supermarkets with a telephone or video link to remote staff. Customer reaction to these is not wholly positive, but they can give some continued service in areas where branches have closed or never existed. Another type of banking machine uses personal telephone or interactive television. Customers can use these directly from home – or any other convenient location – and video links can give virtual face-to-face contact.

Smartcards, which use an embedded chip to store a range of personal information, will automate even more bank transactions. Unfortunately, there can be problems with the security of these cards, as the current PIN number system can easily be abused. Many machines use a pin-hole camera to take a picture of the person using the card. Early experiments tried to link this picture with a stored photograph of the person authorized to use the card, but with limited success. A more reliable alternative of 'iris identification' was tested in 1998 by the Nationwide Building Society. This uses a machine to scan the user's eye and compare the iris with a recorded version. As the computer can then identify the customer, there is really no need for the smartcard and a customer only has to stand in front of a machine, be recognized, and carry out any transactions automatically. This instant identification also solves another problem with cards, as most systems cannot deal profitably with a transaction of less than about £25. Most purchases are less than this, so there is still a significant amount of dealing with cash. Automatic identification will allow even small electronic transactions, and might eventually do away completely with the need for cash.

CHOOSING THE RIGHT LEVEL OF TECHNOLOGY

High technology can increase the productivity of a process and bring other benefits, but this does not mean that every organization should immediately replace its current process with a high-technology alternative. Many other factors have to be considered, the most obvious being capital costs. Unless the process makes high volumes, the capital costs are spread over too few units and the unit cost is prohibitive.

Apart from cost, there are several other factors to consider. Higher levels of automation can reduce the flexibility of a process, and may create a barrier between customers and the final product. This is the reason why people using a tourist information office walk past computerized information systems and talk directly to a person behind the desk. However, perhaps the major criticism of automated systems is that they ignore the skills that people can bring, including:

- giving a personal service;
- drawing upon varied experiences;
- intelligent use of all available information;
- use of subjectivity and judgement;
- ability to adapt to new and unusual circumstances;
- generate entirely new solutions;
- recognizing patterns; and
- using creativity.

On the other hand, machines have the following advantages:

- they work continuously without tiring;
- they give reliable – often higher – quality;
- they are fast and powerful;
- they do many tasks at the same time;
- they store and process large amounts of information;
- they do dangerous or boring jobs; and
- they save on operating costs.

People and machines are better at different jobs, and because automation is sometimes useful you should not assume that it is better for everything.

Management example – electronic dealing at Liffe

The London International Financial Futures Exchange (Liffe) was formed in 1982 to enable companies to offset the negative impact of sharp fluctuations in currencies. It had a huge open dealing floor where 2,000 traders, wearing multi-coloured jackets, worked in trading pits. Deals were made using a combination of shouting and hand signals. This apparently chaotic system was one of the most successful markets in the City, with contracts of £160 billion traded every day.

By 1998, however, the 'open-outcry' system was showing signs of strain, and some of the big banks were pressing for change. Lloyds TSB pulled out of trading on the floor, Nikko reduced its presence, and SBC Warburg stopped trading German Government bonds. The alternative to open trading is computer-based dealing, with operators sitting at terminals. This system was used in Frankfurt, which was rapidly taking over from London as the European centre for financial futures.

Screen trading has been used by the London Stock Exchange for years, and this has the advantage of being cheaper to run and more efficient. The screen system of Frankfurt, for example, cost 30 per cent less than the open system in London. On the other hand, the screen system could be inflexible, and poor at dealing with unusual deals, and would favour big traders over the locals – individuals who deal for their own account and make up about 30 per cent of Liffe business.

In May 1998, Liffe voted to move to screen dealing, with a residual open system for contracts that are not easily adapted to screen-based systems, such as Euromark contracts with short-term interest rates. The decision to change was needed quickly, as Liffe was due to move from Cannon Street in the City, to a proposed new £300 million headquarters in Spitalfields, which included a trading floor of 100,000 square feet. The change to screen-trading made this floor unnecessary, and the 220 members who owned the mutual exchange eventually decided not to move.

LAYOUTS FOR DIFFERENT TYPES OF PROCESS

Another important decision in the design of a process concerns the physical arrangement of equipment, offices, and other resources. In a Sainsbury's supermarket, goods are arranged in parallel aisles. This layout, which is designed to encourage customers to buy goods, is the result of much experience and experimentation.

Every organization has to consider the layout of its operations, whether it is an office, manufacturer, warehouse, or government debating chamber. Facilities that are well laid out are efficient and allow a smooth flow of work through the process; poorly laid out facilities are inefficient and disrupt operations. The difference is seen in, say, airport terminals; some can handle large numbers of passengers very efficiently, while others have queues, crowds milling around, and people wandering around obviously lost.

There are basically five different types of layout:

- process;
- product;
- hybrid;
- fixed position; and
- specialized.

Process layouts

In a process layout, all similar types of operations are grouped together. Hospitals use a process layout and put all equipment for emergencies in one ward, surgical patients in another, and paediatrics in another. A job shop might put all drilling machines in one area, grinders in another area, and milling machines in a third area. This layout works best when different products use the same resources, and every product follows a different route through them (as shown in Figure 5.3).

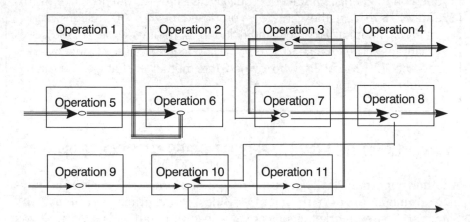

Figure 5.3 *Process layout, with similar operations grouped together and products following different paths*

Offices often use a process layout, with people working in groups according to their skills – accountants work in one area, lawyers in another, planners in a third. These can form cohesive groups that work together well, giving both high morale and productivity.

Product layouts

A product layout groups together all the operations used to make a particular product. This is the basis of an assembly or production line, in which all the equipment is lined up in order and each unit of the product passes straight down the line (as shown in Figure 5.4). There is an obvious link between product layouts and mass production processes.

The process uses dedicated equipment, and the product moves through this in a steady flow. In principle, product layouts are easy to design, but they need careful planning if a smooth flow and high utilization of all resources are to be achieved.

Hybrid layouts

Often the best layout is not a pure process layout, or a pure product layout, but some combination of the two. A 'work cell' is an example of a common hybrid layout, in which there is a dominant process layout, but some operations are set aside in a product layout. This might be seen in a factory, where most machines will be laid out in a job shop, but where a certain sequence of operations is repeated so often that a special area, or work cell, is set aside to deal with those operations on an assembly line. Some examples of this are:

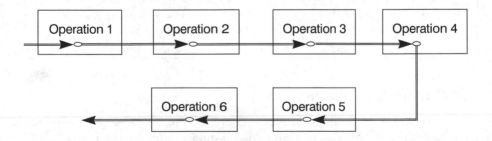

Figure 5.4 *Product layout, with all operations taken in order*

- An airport passenger terminal has a process layout with separate ticket purchase area, check-in area, cafeteria, duty free shops, and so on. Despite this, there are some product layouts, such as customs clearance.
- A fast-food restaurant has areas of the kitchen set aside for different purposes, but a line that prepares all hamburgers.
- A hospital has wards set aside for different types of illness, but the patient admissions area has a product layout.

The idea of a work centre can be extended to focused factories, where the work centre is moved to another building. In this case, a focused factory uses a product layout to make components or products for use in another facility.

Management example – Dalmuir Knitwear

Dalmuir Knitwear makes fairly small numbers of fashion garments, mainly for women but with some sportswear for men. It weaves, knits, dyes, sews, assembles and finishes a range of clothing. Because of the fairly small production quantities, Dalmuir uses a process layout, with a weaving room, knitting room, finishing room, and so on.

Two years ago the company won a large contract to supply garments to Marks & Spencer. This was a major success for Dalmuir, which was pleased that it could meet Marks & Spencer's extremely high standards. Because these standards required a higher quality than their usual operations, Dalmuir set aside a special area of their factory solely to make the Marks & Spencer order. This area was completely refurbished and equipped with their latest machines. The machines were arranged in a product layout, so that the Marks & Spencer products were moved in a straight line through the factory.

The plant manager at Dalmuir looked after all the operations, and effectively created a special production line to meet this one contract. Any spare capacity in the production line was used to make a new range of high-quality garments for other customers.

Fixed-position layouts

In fixed-position layouts the product stays still and operations are all done on the same site. This usually happens when a product is too big or heavy to move around. Common examples are in shipbuilding, aeroplane assembly and on construction sites. The approach is also useful when special environments, such as dust-free rooms, are needed.

Fixed-position layouts have many disadvantages: all materials have to be moved to the site; there might be limited space, and congestion; the intensity of work varies; the work needs a reliable schedule, but it is prone to disruptions and delays, and can be influenced by external factors such as the weather. Because of these disadvantages, fixed-position layouts are only used when moving the product is either impossible or very difficult. One way to avoid some of these disadvantages is to do as much of the work as possible off-site. With a road bridge, for example, many of the parts can be prefabricated off-site and then moved to the final site for erection.

Specialized layouts

There are many examples of specialized layouts, including warehouses that store goods at some point on their journey between suppliers and customers. Such a warehouse will consist of:

- an arrival bay, where goods coming from suppliers are delivered and checked;
- a storage area, where the goods are kept as stock;
- a departure bay, where customers' orders are assembled and sent out;
- a material-handling system, for moving goods around; and
- an information system, which records all transactions and other relevant information.

Finding the best design for a warehouse – and other specialized layouts such as offices, shops, schools and airports – requires specialized skills and considerable expertise.

CHAPTER REVIEW

- The process describes the detailed operations needed to make a product. Process planning finds the best possible process for a product.
- The process plays an important part in an organization's ability to compete. Many organizations have recognized this and have become process-centred.
- Processes can be classified as project, job shop, batch, mass production or continuous flow. Each of these has different characteristics and is best suited to different types of products.
- A number of factors are important in choosing the best process, including product design, demand, variation in demand, flexibility needed, quality, finances, workforce skills, and stage in the product life cycle.

- Different levels of automation are classified as manual, mechanized or automated. Higher levels of technology generally give higher productivity, but organizations should choose the level of automation that best suits the design of the product.
- The layout of a process should be designed to make it as efficient as possible. Alternatives include product, process, hybrid, fixed position and specialized layouts.

FURTHER READING

Benders, J, DeHaan, J and Bennett, D (eds) (1995) *The Symbiosis of Work and Technology*, Taylor and Francis, London

Gunton, T (1990) *Inside Information Technology: A practical guide to management issues*, Prentice Hall, Englewood Cliffs, NJ

Hammer, M (1996) *Beyond Re-engineering*, Harper Collins, London

Ramaswamy, R (1996) *Design and Management of Service Process*, Addison Wesley Longman, Harlow

Wu, B (1994) *Manufacturing Systems Design and Analysis* (2nd edition), Chapman and Hall, New York

CHAPTER 6

Planning for the Process

RESOURCE PLANNING

Chapter 5 looked at the design of processes, including the basic decisions relating to the overall type of process, the level of technology and the layout. At this stage, the detailed planning of the process needs to be looked at. The first essential is to make sure that there is enough capacity to meet long-term forecast demand. If the organization has to increase capacity, it might have to build new facilities; on the other hand, reducing capacity might lead to staff lay-offs and the closing of facilities. These are strategic decisions with effects in the long term.

When the available capacity matches the forecast demand, the organization has to design a timetable to show exactly when it will make the products. This production plan must meet the long-term demand, allow for variations in demand over the shorter term, and keep within the available capacity. This production plan then gives timetables for employees, equipment, material purchases and other operations. At this point, the plans have moved down from strategic capacity plans and on to detailed operational schedules (as shown in Figure 6.1).

There is some disagreement about the terms used to describe the different levels of planning, but we will refer to them as follows:

- 'capacity plans', which make sure that there is enough overall capacity to meet the long-term demand;
- 'aggregate plans', which show the overall production for families of products, typically by month at each location;
- 'master production schedules', which show a detailed timetable of production for each product, typically by week; and
- 'short-term schedules', which show detailed timetables for jobs, equipment, people and other resources, typically by day.

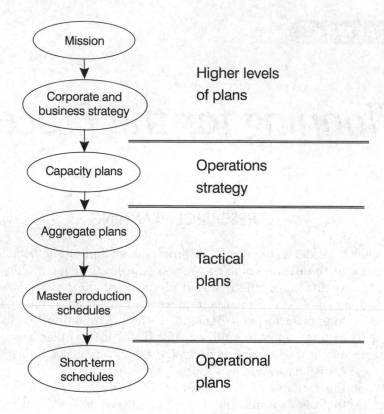

Figure 6.1 *Levels of planning for the process*

Management example – Allenby Tools

Allenby Tools make a variety of garden tools in three factories. One run of their 1999 planning procedure is summarized as follows.

- Strategic plan – making the fundamental decisions. The Board of Directors, with George Allenby as its Chairman, decided to continue making garden tools of high quality and using appropriate processes. They continue operations in three factories at Gateshead, Bradford and Exeter.
- Capacity plan – examining long-term forecasts of demand and adjusting capacity to meet these.
- Long-term forecasts show a demand for 50,000 garden tools a year, which means there is a shortage of capacity of 10,000 tools a year. Jane Lucas, the Operations Director, decides to overcome this shortage by increasing the staff in Exeter and working two shifts at

Bradford. Then forecast demand can be met as follows: Gateshead making 10,000 tools a year; Bradford making 20,000 tools a year; Exeter making 20,000 tools a year.

■ Aggregate plan – breaking down the capacity plan into monthly plans for each location. The three plant managers get together, look at the capacity plans, and design aggregate plans to meet these. Gateshead makes 1,000 tools in January; Bradford makes 2,500 tools in January; and so on.

■ Master production schedule – breaking down the aggregate plan into weekly plans for individual products. George Thirkettle, the Plant Manager at Gateshead, passes the aggregate plan to Mary Wilson who designs the master production schedules:

Gateshead   Schedule for January
Week 1:   make 100 spades, 50 forks, 100 rakes
Week 2:   make 50 spades, 250 rakes
Week 3:   make 100 spades, 100 rakes, and so on.

■ Short-term schedules – breaking down the master production schedule into daily timetables for individual batches of tools and equipment. Mary Wilson passes the master production schedule to her assistants, who design detailed daily schedules.

Gateshead, January, Week 1: Monday morning shift – 10 spades on machines 1 to 4; 10 rakes on machines 5 to 8. Monday afternoon shift – 20 forks on machines 1 to 8. Tuesday morning shift: 10 spades on machines 1 to 4; 10 forks on machines 5 to 8, and so on.

CAPACITY OF A PROCESS

Capacity is usually thought of in terms of the volume that something will hold – the capacity of a bottle of wine is 70cl, and the capacity of a theatre is 650 seats. However, in operations terms, 'capacity' defines the maximum amount of a product that can be made in a specified time. If an enquiry desk takes 5 minutes to deal with a customer, it has a capacity of 12 customers an hour. The capacity of a factory is its maximum output a week, the capacity of a restaurant is the maximum number of customers it can seat in an evening, an aeroplane has a maximum number of seats on a flight, a hotel has a maximum number of beds for the night, and a lorry has a maximum weight it can carry on a journey. Capacity measures the rate of output, and should always refer to some relevant time period.

- The capacity of a process is the maximum amount of a product that can be made in a given time under normal working conditions.
- Capacity planning includes all decisions about the capacity of a process.

Sometimes, the capacity of an operation seems obvious – the number of seats in a theatre, or beds in a hospital, or tables in a restaurant. At other times, the capacity is not so clear. How, for example, is it possible to work out the capacity of a supermarket, warehouse, university or bank? It is particularly difficult to find out the capacity of such services, and some surrogate measure is often used, such as the number of customers per square metre of floor space. These measures are usually found by discussion and agreement rather than by calculation. The maximum size of classes in schools, for example, is an agreed number of pupils rather than some limit set by the building. The maximum number of spectators in a football stadium is set by agreed safety regulations, rather than by physical limitations of space.

APPROACH TO CAPACITY PLANNING

In principle, capacity planning is simple. All that is needed is a forecast of long-term demand, and then enough capacity is built to meet this demand.

- If we build less capacity, we cannot meet all the demand and lose potential customers.
- If we build more capacity, we can meet all the demand but will have spare capacity and the extra costs of under-used resources.

Sometimes, a customer may go into a shop where there are not enough people serving, and will have to wait. The capacity of the shop is less than the demand, and the customer will probably go to a competitor where the queues are shorter. In other shops, there are many people waiting to serve, so the customer does not have to wait, but the cost of paying these under-used people is added to the customer's bill.

In practice, of course, things are not this simple. The amount of product made by a process can vary quite widely, depending on how hard people work, the number of interruptions, the quality needed, the efficiency of equipment, pressure exerted by managers, and a range of other factors. Also most organizations do not like to work at full capacity, as equipment becomes less reliable, people feel over-stretched, and there is no cushion to deal with sudden changes or unexpected events.

The capacity of a process is its maximum output when it is working normally. Designers often think of ideal conditions, in which everything works well and there are no problems, interruptions, maintenance, or other stoppages; so the designed capacity is the maximum output under ideal conditions. Processes rarely work under ideal conditions, so the effective capacity is a more realistic measure, which can be expected under normal conditions. The designed capacity of a ski lift, for example, might be 600 people an hour, but, because some seats are not filled, because people arrive in groups, and because there are interruptions as people have problems getting on and off, the effective capacity might only be 400 people an hour.

Not all of the effective capacity of a process is used, because of the way that products use different amounts of the available resources. One product might use all the available supply of a resource – perhaps time on one machine – and this forms a bottleneck. At this point, this machine is working at full capacity, but all the other resources have spare capacity. (For more on this idea of capacity utilization, see Chapter 10.)

Operations that form the bottlenecks limit the capacity of the overall process. If Jameson Restaurant can cook 200 meals in an evening, but can only seat 100 customers, the bottleneck that limits capacity is the seating. If Wendy Jones Associates can make 30 gold brooches a week, but can only afford to buy enough gold for 20, the overall capacity is set by the supply of gold. The only way of increasing capacity is to slacken the constraint on the bottleneck. Jameson Restaurant can only increase capacity by adding more seats, and improving the kitchen will have no effect at all on capacity. Although this seems obvious, there are many everyday cases in which people do not identify where the real constraints apply. For example, organizations recruit more managers to give leadership, when they are actually short of workers to do the jobs; companies increase the size of customer waiting areas, when they should be serving customers faster; manufacturers recruit more salespeople, when current production is too low and is giving long lead times.

Management example – Trivistor Soft Drinks

Trivistor Soft Drinks has a bottling hall consisting of the following automatic bottling, labelling and packing machines.

Table 6.1 *Machines in Trivistor bottling hall*

Type of machine	Bottling	Labelling	Packing
Number of machines	2	3	1
Capacity per machine	100 litres per min.	3,000 bottles an hr	10,000 cases a day
Total designed capacity	200 litres per min.	9,000 bottles an hr	10,000 cases a day
Total designed capacity in bottles a day	200 x 60 x 12 =144,000	9,000 x 12 = 108,000	10,000 x 12 =120,000
Effective capacity in bottles a day	112,000	97,000	101,500

The capacity of the whole bottling hall is set by the labelling machines, which can only handle 97,000 bottles a day. Both the bottling and packing machines have spare capacity.

Management example – Heathrow Airport

BAA runs the major UK airports. In the year to April 1998, the authority handled 104.5 million passengers, an increase of 6.7 per cent over the previous year. Passenger demand is particularly strong in the south-east of England, where the number of passengers is forecast to double over the next 15 years. To meet this rising demand, BAA has a continuing programme of airport expansion.

London Heathrow is the world's biggest international airport, and in the year to 1998 handled 58 million passengers. This rise of 3.6 per cent for the year was modest compared with other airports around London. Gatwick, Stansted and Luton airports grew by over 12 per cent, while the smaller London City Airport recently doubled traffic to a million passengers a year.

The reason for Heathrow's relatively slow growth is that the runways and four terminals are already working at full capacity. Passenger growth only really comes from bigger planes and increasing occupancy. There are plans to add a fifth terminal at Heathrow and to increase passenger capacity to 85 million a year, but the public enquiry into the new terminal took over three years to report – the longest-ever hearing for a development project in the UK. Any new terminal is unlikely to be finished before 2005. None the less, developments are going ahead to give smaller increases in capacity, including a new express rail link to London Paddington, a second express rail link to St Pancras in Central London, wider access roads, a further extension to the London Underground Piccadilly Line, and £1 million a day spent on upgrading the existing four terminals. Discussions are also starting to reduce the gap between aeroplanes, and so allow more take-offs and landings.

Realistically, the congestion at Heathrow is likely to continue for the foreseeable future. This has forced growth at other airports, and the effects of this can be seen at, say, Gatwick Airport to the south of London. British Airways switched its African services to Gatwick in 1996, and its South American services in 1997. By 1998, Gatwick was serving 276 destinations – more than any other European gateway, including Heathrow. It spent £500 million to increase its capacity from 27 million to 30 million passengers. Similar effects are felt at the other London airports, with knock-on effects at more distant British airports such Southampton, Glasgow and Edinburgh.

CAPACITY PLANNING

Capacity planning is largely a strategic function. The capacity of a process might be increased by building another facility or changing the process; spare capacity can be reduced by closing down facilities or using them for other products. These are major decisions, which will have long-term effects on the organization. Other aspects of capacity planning are shorter term. Capacity might be increased by renting extra space, or by working overtime for a spell; these are tactical and operational decisions. The objective of capacity planning is to make sure that capacity matches forecast demand over the long term, with shorter-term adjustments to allow for variations in demand or any other mismatches.

The aim of capacity planning is to match available capacity to forecast demand over the long, medium and short term.

There is a standard approach to capacity planning, in which planners have to do the following:

1. examine forecast demand and translate this into a capacity requirement;
2. calculate the available capacity of present facilities;
3. identify mismatches between capacity needs and availability;
4. generate alternative plans for overcoming any mismatch;
5. compare these alternative plans and choose the best;
6. implement the best plan – then check and control its progress.

This process is sometimes called 'resource requirement planning'. Unfortunately, taking the steps in this straightforward sequence does not usually work. In most circumstances, there are a huge number of possible plans, and it is impossible to look at all of them in detail. It is also difficult to compare the alternatives, as there is a range of competing objectives and non-quantifiable factors. A more realistic view replaces the single procedure with an iterative one. This designs a plan and sees how close it gets to achieving its objectives; if it performs badly, the plan is modified and again assessed. Steps 4 and 5 in the planning procedure are repeated until they give a satisfactory result.

This iterative procedure recognizes that it is usually impossible to find the single 'best' plan, and that what is really being sought is one that is generally accepted. Plans that appeal to the marketing department may be very inefficient for operations; the best plans for operations may not suit personnel; the best plans for personnel may be too expensive for finance. A compromise is always needed between conflicting objectives and subjective views. This compromise must consider many factors, including:

- demand – forecast sales; sales already made; back orders; variation in demand;
- operations – machine capacity and utilization; aim of stable production; plans for new equipment; use of subcontractors; productivity targets;
- materials – availability of raw materials; inventory policies; current inventory levels; constraints on storage;
- finance – costs; cash flows; financing arrangements; exchange rates; general economic climate;
- human resources – workforce levels; levels of skills and productivity; unemployment rates; hiring and training policies;
- marketing – reliability of forecasts; competition; plans for new products; product substitution.

Finding a reasonable balance between these factors is difficult, and the iterative planning procedure may be repeated many times before a plan is finally accepted.

PERIOD COVERED BY PLANS

The planning procedure gives a set of plans for a specific period, but planning is continuous and never-ending. As plans for one period are finalized and implemented, planners move on to consider the next period, so they are really designing a series of plans, one for every period. This makes planning much easier, as plans for one period can be used as a basis for future plans, and the organization can work in cycles. In one cycle, planners might design definite plans for the next period, tentative plans for the following period, and outline plans for the period after that (as shown in Figure 6.2). It is difficult to generalize, but strategic plans might cover the next five years, and be updated annually. Aggregate plans might cover the next six months and be updated every three months. Obviously, the further ahead the plans look, the more tentative they are, while closer plans are finalized and form the basis of lower-level schedules.

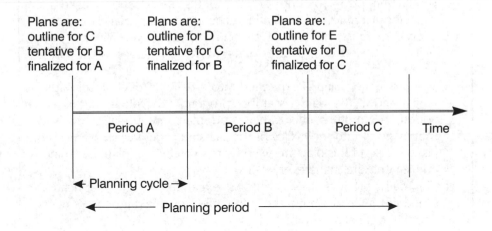

Figure 6.2 *Continual updating of plans in cycles*

Management example – Kawasaki Heavy Industries

Kawasaki Heavy Industries is probably best known for its motorcycles, which are made in a number of plants around the world. Production planning at these plants is derived from inputs from several sources, including forecasts of local demand, and the requirements of the main plant in Akashi, Japan. Kawasaki's current planning process is outlined below, but the company looks for continuous improvements and makes frequent changes.

- The process starts with a sales forecast, which gives the monthly demand for each model of motor cycle for the next year. This is updated every 3 months.
- The forecasts are consolidated into a sales plan, which shows the number of each model that must be available for sale each month for the next year. The plan is updated every 3 months, with the final 3 months considered firm.
- The sales plan is one input to the production plan at plants. This production plan looks up to 18 months ahead and is used for capacity planning and budgeting. The production plan is updated every 3 months, with the last 3 months fixed to agree with the sales plan. Scheduled deliveries of parts allow no changes in the last 6 weeks.
- The production plan is expanded into a daily production schedule, which shows the daily assembly programme. Details of this are added 4–5 months in advance, and plans are updated every 3 months to fit into the cycles of the sales and production plans. The last 6 weeks of this plan are fixed by the production plan, but minor adjustments are made every week.
- The daily production schedule is expanded to give fabrication schedules, which show the timetable for making components needed for final assembly.
- The fabrication schedules are expanded to find the purchase orders needed to get parts and materials from suppliers.

ADJUSTMENTS TO CAPACITY

Capacity planning is largely a strategic function, but the process must have enough flexibility to allow for short-term adjustments. Suppose that a local radio station has two people answering telephone calls from the public. This sets the normal capacity, but the station might hire part-time staff to increase capacity during a particularly popular phone-in programme. Some people say that such short-term mismatches between supply and demand are inevitable, and they happen with even the most careful planning. However, they often show that the organization simply has not done its planning properly and has made some serious mistakes. When the Parisian Bijou Cinema offered a 'nostalgia night', cutting the admission price to half a crown (12.5 pence), it had 950 people queueing for the 7.30 performance; unfortunately, the cinema has only 240 seats.

There are two ways of correcting short-term mismatches between supply and demand: demand management and capacity management.

Demand management

Demand management makes short-term adjustments to demand so that it matches available capacity. Many organizations adjust demand simply by changing prices, but the prices must be high enough to cover all costs, low enough to compare with competitors, and not change so often that customers are confused. There are several ways of adjusting demand, including:

- varying the price – with increases for products with too little capacity and decreases for products with spare capacity;
- changing the marketing effort;
- offering incentives, such as discounts for off-peak telephone calls or travel, or free samples of products with spare capacity;
- changing related products, so they can substitute for products in short supply;
- keeping spare units in stock to be used later;
- varying the lead time, making customers wait for products in short supply;
- using a reservation or appointment system.

One unusual effect of demand management is that organizations may actively discourage customers at times of high demand. At first this seems strange, but it is really quite common. Professional institutions put up barriers against newcomers wanting to enter; discotheques have queues outside to stop too many people going in at busy times; expensive cars offer long delivery times; artists make limited editions of prints; and perfume houses charge very high prices in order to discourage mass sales.

Capacity management

Capacity management makes short-term adjustments to capacity so that it matches forecast demand. The obvious way of doing this is to change the working time, using overtime to increase capacity or short time to reduce it. Other ways of adjusting capacity include:

- changing the total hours worked in any period, by changing the number of shifts;
- scheduling work patterns so the total workforce available at any time varies with demand;
- employing part-time staff to cover peak demand;
- using outside contractors, or renting extra space;
- adjusting the process, perhaps making larger batches to reduce set-up times;
- adjusting equipment and processes to work faster or more slowly;
- re-scheduling maintenance periods;
- making the customer do some work, such as using automatic cash-dispensing machines in banks or packing their own bags in supermarkets.

All these short-term adjustments to capacity have associated costs, and they cannot be made too often or too severely. Many of the alternatives affect employees – they are asked to work overtime, shifts, flexible hours or part-time – and such arrangements cannot be changed every few days. Neither can extra space be rented for a few hours at a time. The obvious implication is that a process runs most smoothly with a steady output rather than with wide variations (see later in this chapter).

Problems matching capacity and demand

There are several specific problems in matching capacity and demand. A common difficulty is that demand comes in small quantities and can take on almost any value, while capacity comes in large, discrete amounts. Typically, capacity can be increased by, for example, opening another shop, employing another person, building another factory, using another machine, or buying another vehicle. This makes it very difficult to match capacity exactly to demand.

The Penhale Equestrian Centre has horse-boxes to move customers' horses around the country. Demand for these moves is rising steadily, and at some point Penhale will have to buy more boxes and hire more drivers. This increase in capacity comes in discrete steps, so there is inevitably some mismatch with the continuous demand. There is no way of avoiding this problem, but there are three strategies for dealing with it, as shown in Figure 6.3:

- capacity can more or less match demand, so that sometimes there is spare capacity and sometimes a shortage;
- capacity can be made at least equal to demand at all times, which needs more investment in facilities and gives lower utilization;

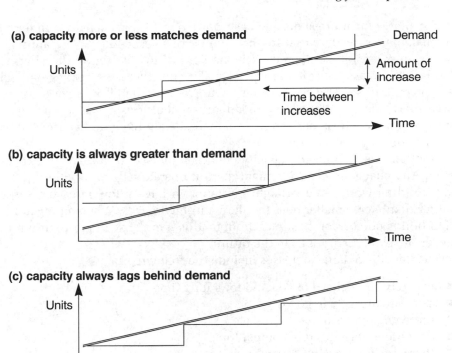

Figure 6.3 *Options for timing of capacity increases*

- capacity can be delayed and only added when it would be fully used, which needs lower investment and gives high utilization, but restricts output.

Each of these strategies is best in different circumstances. The following are some factors that encourage organizations to increase capacity early – as shown in Figure 6.3(b):

- uneven or variable demand;
- high profits, perhaps for a new product;
- high cost of unmet demand, possibly with lost sales;
- a continuously changing product mix;
- uncertainty in capacity or variable efficiency;
- capacity increases that are relatively small;
- low cost of spare capacity, which might be used for other work;
- a need for dependable and flexible operations.

On the other hand, the main factor that makes organizations delay an increase in capacity until the last possible moment – as shown in Figure 6.3(c) – is the capital cost.

For a large furniture shop, such as Courts or MFI, the capacity – in terms of customers served – is set by the number of salespeople. These are relatively inexpensive compared with the cost of lost sales, so the shop is likely to increase capacity early and make sure there are always enough salespeople to serve every customer. On the other hand, it is very expensive to increase the capacity of an urban motorway, so expansion is delayed for as long as possible, and new roads are likely to be crowded as soon as they open.

Another question about capacity concerns the size of a planned expansion. Any change in capacity might disrupt operations – especially if there are building works – so it might be better to have a few large increases rather than more smaller ones (as shown in Figure 6.4). When an organization builds offices, for example, it often adds more space than it currently needs, to avoid disruptions in the future.

The benefits of large increases include the following:

- capacity stays ahead of demand for a long time;
- sales are unlikely to be lost;
- there might be economies of scale;
- operations stay ahead of competitors;
- there are less frequent disruptions.

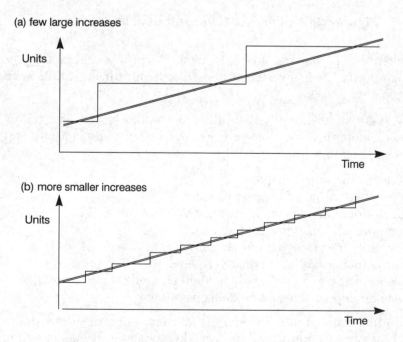

Figure 6.4 *Options for size of capacity increases*

Management example – hospital security

Queen Elizabeth Hospital has a security force of 26 people. They are responsible for the general security of the four hospital buildings and the 7-hectare site. There are very few serious problems, but a few months ago there were three unrelated incidents that raised concerns. When local newspapers published details of these incidents, people started to demand more security. The hospital managers saw this as an operations problem and passed the demands on to the Facility Operations Manager (FOC).

The FOC increased the number of patrols and put more security people in places where they were clearly visible. He also improved the camera surveillance system and experimented with better identity cards for staff and patients. There were no further incidents, but the security people were now working an average of 14 hours a week overtime. After a spell they became tired, and morale dropped. The FOC knew that the security people could not continue to work at this level, so he made a request for five more full-time staff and six part-time staff.

Hospital managers were trying to cut overheads, and were reluctant to divert money away from direct medical care. They thought the problem was temporary and would solve itself if they waited a short time.

On the other hand, the disadvantages include the following:

■ capacity does not match demand so closely;
■ disruptions may be serious;
■ there are high capital costs;
■ utilization will be low;
■ there is high risk if demand changes;
■ the policy is less flexible.

Changing capacity over time

Another problem for planners is that the capacity of a process changes over time. Even if no changes are made to the process, there will be short-term variations due to operator illness, interruptions, breakdowns, or other problems. There are also longer-term changes in capacity, due to effects such as learning curves and equipment deterioration.

Repetition makes activities easier, which is why musicians and sportsmen spend such a long time practising to improve their skills. This effect can be seen in almost all operations, where the time needed to complete a job decreases as the number of repetitions increases. This effect is the learning curve, which raises productivity over time.

Management example – maintenance of cranes

Maintenance of equipment can have a major effect on its reliability and on the cost of operations. Organizations that try to save money on maintenance often find themselves with high bills for breakdowns and disruptions. Each organization has to find the best level of maintenance and replacement for its own operations, but sometimes there are agreed procedures. There is, for example, an international agreement for the maintenance of cranes.

ISO TC 96/SC 5 is the international standard for the maintenance of cranes. Case studies at paper mills in Canada, Finland, Sweden and the United States show that the procedures described in this standard reduced annual maintenance costs by between 33 and 64 per cent, the number of defects by between 46 and 60 per cent, and the number of production failures by between 33 and 97 per cent.

Similar studies in steel mills in Sweden, Canada and the United States reduced annual maintenance costs by between 28 and 56 per cent, the number of defects by between 50 and 83 per cent, and the number of production failures by between 63 and 95 per cent.

Other factors make productivity fall over time, and one of these is the ageing of equipment. As equipment gets older, it breaks down more often, develops more faults, gives lower-quality output, slows down, and generally wears out. Sometimes this change is slow – like the oil consumption of a car, which rises over a period of years. Sometimes the change is very fast, like a bolt that suddenly breaks. A way of avoiding this decline uses routine maintenance to repair equipment at regular intervals, like the 5,000-mile services of a car. As worn bits are replaced, the equipment is restored to give continuing, satisfactory performance.

AGGREGATE PLANS

Aggregate plans and master production schedules bridge the gap between strategic capacity plans and operational details. Aggregate planning takes the forecast demand and planned capacity, and uses them to design a production plan for each family of products, typically for each of the next few months. Aggregate plans only look at the production of *families* of products and are not concerned with individual products. A knitwear manufacturer, for example, makes jumpers and skirts in different styles, colours, and sizes. The aggregate plan only shows the total production of jumpers and the total production of skirts; it does not look in any more detail at the production of a particular style, colour or size. Aggregate plans look at the total number of barrels of beer to brew, or books to print, but not the number of barrels of each type of beer or the number of copies of each title.

Aggregate planning makes the tactical decisions that translate forecast demand and planned capacity into production schedules for families of products.

The main inputs to aggregate plans are the forecast demand and capacity, but there are several other important inputs, including known orders, stock levels, safety stocks, desired service levels, internal demands, and other production constraints. The aggregate plans have to look at these, and answer questions such as the following:

- Should production be kept at a constant level, or changed to meet varying demand?
- Should stocks be used to meet changing demand, producing for stock during periods of low demand and using the accumulated stocks during periods of high demand?
- Should subcontractors be used for peak demands?
- Should the size of the workforce or patterns of work change with demand?
- Should prices be changed?
- Are shortages allowed, perhaps with late delivery?
- Can demand be smoothed?

An important question here concerns the amount of variation in production levels – should production change with demand, or should it be more stable? There are obvious advantages in having stable production, including the following:

- planning is easier;
- the flow of products is smoother;
- there are fewer problems with changes;
- there is no need to 'hire and fire' employees;
- employees have regular work patterns;
- larger batch sizes reduce costs;
- stocks can be reduced;
- throughput can be faster;
- experience with a product reduces problems.

Although a stable production offers many advantages, this is not always the best option. It might be cheaper for a manufacturer to vary production than to keep high stocks of finished goods to meet varying demand; a bus service will vary its schedule to match customer demand, rather than running a fixed number of buses every hour. An organization has to choose between the three basic policies for meeting uneven demand:

- Produce at a constant rate – keeping production constant at the average demand for the planning period. Since the production rate is constant and demand is variable, the differences are met by using stocks, making customers queue, or a similar arrangement.
- Chase demand – having production exactly match demand. This gives no stocks, but the organization has to change production levels every period. This is often the only possible approach for services that cannot store their products.
- Mixed policy – a combination of the first two policies. There are some changes in production rate, but not every period. The policy tries to compromise by having a fairly stable production, but allowing some flexibility for changes. In practice, this is the most common plan.

It is clear that a reasonable objective for aggregate planning is to devise medium-term schedules for families of products, which allow all demand to be met, keep production relatively stable, keep within the constraints of the capacity plan, and meet any other specific objectives and constraints. There are several ways of designing such plans, as follows.

Intuitive approach

Like most plans, aggregate plans are not usually designed from scratch, but are variations on previous plans. As next month's production will be similar to last month's, the easiest approach is to ask an experienced planner to review the current situation and, in the light of experiences with similar plans, to design an updated version. This is a very common way of planning, and has the benefits of convenience and ease of use; also, it involves a well-understood process, and experts can give results that are trusted by the organization. Unfortunately, the results may have a variable and uncertain quality, the plan may take a long time to design, relying solely on the skills of the planner, and it can include bias.

Graphical methods

Planners often find it easier to visualize a plan with a graph, and the most popular format draws a graph of cumulative demand over time, and then adds an aggregate plan as the line of cumulative supply. The aim is to get the cumulative supply line nearly straight – giving constant production – and as close as possible to the cumulative demand line. The advantages of such graphical approaches are that they are easy to use and understand, but they are only one step better than intuitive methods.

Expert systems

These specialized programs use a series of rules to try to duplicate the thinking of a skilled scheduler. Although expert systems have been developing for many years, their results are often disappointing. They can be difficult to design, and require a lot of expertise if they are to work properly.

Spreadsheet calculations

In order to compare a number of alternative plans, it is often easiest to do the calculations in a spreadsheet. A common format lists the resources down the left-hand side, the time periods across the top, available capacity down the right-hand side, and the demand across the bottom. The body of the matrix contains two values: the cost of using resources and the amount of resources actually used. Such spreadsheets are sometimes difficult to design, but they can be very useful for quickly comparing a number of alternative plans.

Simulations

These are more formalized than spreadsheets, and include realistic models of the operations. They follow the process for a typical period and report on its performance. The conditions and values of parameters are then changed to show how different plans perform and how sensitive they are to changes. These can lead to very good results, but it is often difficult to design realistic models.

Mathematical models

A formal, mathematical approach to the problem can give better solutions. Several methods have been proposed for this, usually based on mathematical programming. These have the advantage of the finding an optimal solution – as total costs are minimized or some other objective is achieved. The disadvantages are that they are complicated, difficult to understand, time-consuming, expensive, need a lot of reliable data, and the model still may not be a good description of the real situation.

Specialized software

There is a wide range of software for scheduling, ranging from simple programs using scheduling rules through to expert systems. Most of the suppliers are understandably reluctant to discuss the details of their models. It is fair to say that this software is improving, but it still varies in quality.

MASTER PRODUCTION SCHEDULE

The master production schedule 'dis-aggregates' the aggregate plan and shows the number of individual products to be made in, typically, each week. This gives a detailed timetable of planned output for each product. An aggregate plan for a manufacturer might show 1,000 radiators being made next month, while the master production schedule gives details for each type, with, say, 50 superior radiators and 100 cheaper radiators made in Week 1, 100 superior radiators and 25 cheaper radiators in Week 2, and so on.

- The master production schedule gives a detailed timetable for making individual products.
- This timetable meets the requirements of the aggregate plan as efficiently as possible.

The master production schedule is derived directly from the aggregate plan, so this sets the overall production targets. There might be small differences, to allow for short-term variations, incorrect forecasts and capacity constraints. In particular, the master production schedule is designed relatively close to the start of production, when some orders may already have been received. Then the demand is found from a mixture of:

- production specified by the aggregate plan;
- modifications made by more recent forecasts; and
- customer orders already received.

Some of this demand can be met from stock, so current stock levels, production capacities and a range of other factors must be considered when designing a master production schedule.

In principle, designing a master production schedule is the same as designing an aggregate plan. It is therefore possible to use an intuitive approach, graphical method, spreadsheet, expert system, simulation, mathematical model or specialized software, as before. However, a master production schedule deals with more details, often down to individual customer orders. This makes the planning even more difficult, and it tends to rely more on subjective decisions. Most master production schedules are designed by skilled schedulers, using a range of experience and simple rules.

The planning again occurs in cycles, so schedulers are able to modify previous schedules in order to draw up new versions. This iterative approach, with plans continually adjusted until they are generally accepted, typically takes place up to 3 weeks before the schedule is implemented. The resulting plan is used for scheduling all other operations, so it must be fixed at some point, with no further changes allowed. At that stage, the short-term schedulers can start to design the detailed timetables for people, equipment, raw materials, and other resources. This, the most detailed level of planning, will be discussed in Chapter 7.

CHAPTER REVIEW

- When the overall design of the process has been chosen, an organization must plan the details of the processes. This planning is done at all levels, from strategic through to operational.
- The first stages of planning look at the capacity needed for a process. Capacity planning matches available capacity to forecast demand. This is largely a strategic function, but with some tactical and operational adjustments.
- There is a general procedure for planning. This starts by looking at the forecast demands, and requirements set by the previous level of planning. Any mismatches between supply and demand are identified, and alternative plans for overcoming these mismatches are compared.
- Planning is usually done iteratively, with adjustments made until an acceptable result is found. This procedure recognizes that the planning is difficult, and the results are judged by many factors and need a compromise between competing objectives.
- Aggregate plans add details to the capacity plans and give production schedules for each family of products, typically for each of the next few months. These plans try to meet forecast demand without breaking any constraints, and with relatively stable production.
- There are many ways of approaching the design of aggregate plans, including subjective approaches, graphical methods, spreadsheets, expert systems, simulation, mathematical models and specialized software.
- The master production schedule adds details to the aggregate plans, to give the production of individual products, typically for each of the next few weeks. Designing a master production schedule is similar in principle to designing an aggregate plan, but the increased details can make it more complicated.

FURTHER READING

Goldratt, E and Cox, J (1984) *The Goal*, North River Press, New York

Green, J H (1987) *Production and Inventory Control Handbook* (2nd edition) McGraw-Hill, New York

Menasse, D (1993) *Capacity Planning: A practical approach*, Prentice-Hall, Englewood Cliffs, NJ

Proud, J F (1995) *Master Scheduling*, John Wiley, New York

Vollman, T E, Berry, W L and Whybark, D C. (1992) *Manufacturing Planning and Control Systems* (3rd edition), Richard Irwin, Homewood, Il

CHAPTER 7

Short-term Scheduling

PLANNING AND SCHEDULING

Chapter 6 showed how organizations start to plan resources by making strategic decisions about capacity, and then expand these to draw up tactical aggregate plans and master production schedules. At this point, there is a timetable for making individual products, say, each week. The last stage of planning is to design short-term, operational timetables for each part of the process. This is one of the most common problems in any organization, which looks for:

- the best sequences for operations and jobs;
- consequent timing of each operation;
- a timetable of resources used to support the operations.

Short-term schedules give detailed timetables for jobs, people, equipment, raw material purchases and other resources needed by the process.
They organize the resources to achieve the master production schedule as efficiently as possible.

Every resource used in the process needs a schedule of some kind: staff work scheduled hours; buses and trains have fixed timetables; people schedule meetings; delivery vehicles have drop lists, showing when to visit customers; universities have timetables for classes and rooms; equipment has scheduled use; and factories schedule the arrival of raw materials. Without these schedules, the operations – and the overall process – would be disorganized and chaotic. Therefore, the short-term schedules give detailed timetables for all resources – they show how to achieve the output specified in the master production schedule, while giving low costs and high utilization of equipment, and keeping within all constraints on the process (see Figure 7.1).

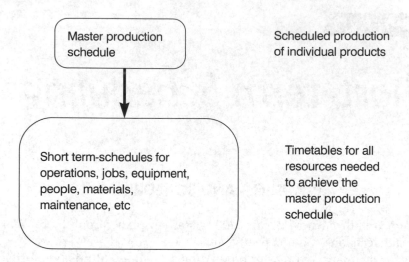

Figure 7.1 *Short-term schedules*

Management example – scheduling at Courtesy Cabs

Courtesy Cabs has a fleet of 110 cars working around Munich. The company employs 165 full-time drivers and a varying number of part-time drivers, usually around 90 but up to 200 during busy periods. The cars only earn money while they are out on the road, so Courtesy tries to keep them working long hours, preferably approaching 24 hours a day.

Courtesy has its own garage where it maintains the fleet. This has four bays, four full-time mechanics, two part-time mechanics and two apprentices. Any spare capacity is used for repairs and maintenance for external customers.

All activities within Courtesy are co-ordinated by eight controllers who design schedules for every part of the organization. They start by scheduling the hours worked by cars, so that there are always enough taxis out on the roads to meet expected demand. Then they schedule drivers, so that the cars always have someone available to drive them. The controllers design routes for each cab, starting with customers who make advance bookings and a list of regular customers who have block bookings. These routes are continually modified as customers telephone in with new jobs, which are assigned to a car that is near by and has enough free time; otherwise, the cars pick up passengers who hail them on the streets.

As well as scheduling the cars, drivers and routes, the controllers design schedules for the maintenance and repair of cars, other internal work in the garage, work for external customers in the garage, hours worked by all other staff, purchase of parts and materials, cleaning and maintenance of the building, staff training, and all other operations of the business.

There are many different aspects of scheduling. It would be easy to spend a long time talking about these in general terms, but it would be more useful to illustrate some specific topics. In order to do this, we will look at three types of problem:

- scheduling jobs on machines;
- scheduling the arrival of materials; and
- scheduling work.

SCHEDULING JOBS ON MACHINES

A standard scheduling problem has a set of jobs waiting to be processed on machines. The aim is to arrange the jobs on the machines so that the work is done as efficiently as possible – perhaps minimizing the waiting time, minimizing the total processing time, keeping stocks low, reducing the maximum lateness, achieving high utilization of equipment, or some other objective. Of course, the terms 'jobs' and 'machines' are used here just for convenience, and this problem really represents many different situations – for example, patients waiting to see doctors in hospital, aeroplanes waiting to land at an airport, applications waiting to run on a computer, or fields waiting for a farmer to work on them.

This may seem an easy problem to resolve, but – as is usual with planning – it is notoriously difficult. This is because of the large number of variables, which typically include the following:

- patterns of job arrivals;
- amount and type of equipment to be used;
- number and skills of operators;
- patterns of work flow through equipment;
- priority of jobs;
- disruptions caused by customer changes, breakdowns, and so on;
- methods of evaluating schedules; and
- objectives of the schedulers.

Managers have tried many approaches to achieve optimal solutions to such scheduling problems – particularly mathematical programming – but most of them are so complicated that they cannot be used for real problems of any size. Despite a huge effort being put into searching for better methods, the most effective way of scheduling is often to use simple rules that give reasonable results. There are hundreds of these rules for different purposes. For example, an approach to the simplest problem, which has jobs waiting to use a single machine, might be to follow some very simple rules to put the jobs in order.

- First-come-first-served. This is the most common scheduling rule, seen in supermarkets, at roundabouts and in many other operations. It is the fairest rule, assuming that all jobs have the same priority and that none is more important than the others. The drawback is that jobs that actually are more urgent can be delayed while less important ones are being processed.
- Most urgent job first. This schedules jobs in order of decreasing urgency. Emergency departments in hospitals, for example, will treat patients who are most seriously in need first. More important jobs are given higher priority, but those jobs that have low priority may get stuck at the end of a very long queue.
- Shortest job first. This rule minimizes the average time spent in the process. Jobs that can be done quickly move on through the system, while longer jobs are left until nearer the end.

Management example – Wrightson Duplication

Wrightson Duplication reproduces any kind of document. Most of its customers are businesses, which bring documents during the working day and want copies within 24 hours. These jobs might need typesetting, formatting, scanning, graphics work, printing, photocopying, collating, stapling, binding, folding, putting in envelopes, or a range of other operations.

Wrightson has about 50 machines that are organized as a job shop. When a job arrives, a receptionist puts it in a standard box, together with a form describing the work to be done, and the route through the machines. This box is put into a queue in front of the first machine it needs and waits for the machine to become free. When the job is finished on one machine, the operator checks it, and passes it to the queue in front of the next machine it needs. This is repeated until the job is sent to a finishing area, where it is checked, costed and left for the customer to pick up.

When Wrightson first opened, the boxes were taken on a first-come-first-served basis. This led to complaints from some customers, especially those with short, urgent jobs that had to wait behind longer, less urgent ones. Wrightson quickly added an order code to each job description, which was based on length of the job, the equipment it needed and the urgency. Taking the jobs in order of this code reduced complaints, but the flow of work was sometimes erratic, and some jobs were left waiting for several days.

Eventually, Wrightson bought a computerized scheduling system from a local consultant. This scans the job description for all new jobs and finds the requirements, length, urgency, customer, and any other relevant information. Then it compares the new job with existing schedules and automatically adds the job to the schedule in the best position. It does this using a hierarchy of scheduling rules that were originally developed in a local factory. Whenever a job leaves one of the machines, an operator updates the computer, which then signals the next job to be done.

This scheduling system virtually eliminated all customer complaints. It also gives a variety of data to managers, who feel it is largely responsible for an increase of 200 per cent in workload over the past 3 years. The computer system cost £40,000 to install and it paid for itself within six months.

Management example – Port of Piraeus

Piraeus in Athens is by far the largest port in Greece. In 1996, it saw 12 million passengers, 10 million tonnes of non-containerized cargo, and 585,000 TEUs ('twenty-foot equivalent units', referring to the standard twenty-foot container). Its income of $120 million a year comes from cargo-handling, port dues, storage, and charges for any other services offered by the port.

Shipping lines work a 'hub-and-spoke' system, with large ships stopping at the hubs, and smaller feeder vessels connecting to local ports. The Mediterranean has a main trunk route from the Suez Canal to Gibraltar, and there are several ports along this route competing for the hub traffic, including Piraeus, Malta, Algeciras in Spain, Damietta in Egypt, and Gioia Tauro in Italy.

In 1996, Piraeus was surprised by a fall of 3 per cent in container traffic, at a time when it was expanding and building new facilities. The port had to make sure that it could generate enough new traffic to justify the expansion. To achieve fast results, it concentrated on the trans-shipment trade, in which shipping lines use the port to move containers between large ships. Then, a number of significant changes were made.

■ With its increased capacity, the port could guarantee arriving ships immediate access to berths and cranes.
■ Trans-shipment tariffs were too high to be competitive, so these were reduced and simplified.
■ Berths had been scheduled on a first-come-first-served basis. The port looked for ways of overriding this in order to give a clearly fair allocation of resources to different types of customers.
■ A booking system was developed, allowing shipping lines to book a time slot and services in advance, and thereby get guaranteed service.
■ The port improved the allocation of cranes and shifts of workers to each ship berthing.
■ Arrangements were improved in the stacking areas, where containers are continually rearranged as they are consolidated for movement to and from ships.
■ Shipping lines were encouraged to consider the benefits of routing ships via Piraeus rather than competing hubs.

As a result of the changes, the container traffic rose to 600,000 TEU in 1997, and to 900,000 TEU in 1998.

Optimised Production Technology (OPT)

Simple scheduling rules can give very good results, but better results often come from more a complicated approach, which typically combines a hierarchy of rules, together with more formal analyses and simulations. One method of scheduling, which has received a lot of attention, was developed by Goldratt, who described the 'theory of constraints'. This concentrates on the capacity constraints, or bottlenecks, in a process, which limit the overall capacity. The only way of increasing production is to remove the bottlenecks. Of course, when one bottleneck is removed, another is created, so this approach is always looking for ways of overcoming the current limiting operation.

Optimised Production Technology (OPT) is a software package based on the ideas of Goldratt; it contains tools that work within the bottlenecks to find efficient schedules. In common with many similar packages, OPT is a proprietary product, and the details of its operations are not published, but it is based on a series of well-known principles.

- Balance the flow through the process rather than the capacity. The production schedule should give the best flow of products through the process and need not keep all resources busy.
- The utilization of operations that are not bottlenecks is not set by its own capacity, but by some other operation in the process.
- Activating a resource (which means doing work that is really needed) is not the same as using the resource (which might include work that is not really needed at the particular time).
- An hour lost at a bottleneck cannot be recovered, and gives an hour lost for the entire process.
- Saving an hour at an operation that is not a bottleneck gives no benefits.
- Bottlenecks control both the throughput of the process and the stocks of work in progress.
- The size of a transfer batch (the number of units moved together between operations) should not equal the size of the process batch (the total number of units made in a production run).
- The size of the process batch should be variable and not fixed.
- Schedules should be designed by looking at constraints simultaneously and not sequentially.
- Lead times are set by the process and cannot be predetermined.
- The sum of local optima is not equal to the optimum of the whole.

SCHEDULING MATERIALS

Another common scheduling problem is the organization of the supply of materials for the process. This is usually viewed as a part of inventory control:

> Stocks are supplies of goods and materials that are held by an organization. Inventory control designs policies to minimize the cost of holding stock.

Stocks are formed whenever the organization's inputs or outputs are not used at the time when they become available. There is almost inevitably some mismatch between supply and use, so all organizations hold stocks of some kind. When a filling station receives a delivery of petrol from a tanker, it is held as stock until it is sold to a customer; when a factory moves finished goods to a warehouse, they are put into stock; when a restaurant buys vegetables, they join the inventory until delivered with a meal to a customer.

There are always costs involved with holding stocks – to cover warehouse operations, tied-up capital, deterioration, insurance, and so on – so an obvious question is, 'Why do organizations hold stock?'. The usual answers to this include:

- to act as a buffer between different operations;
- to allow for demands that are larger than expected, or at unexpected times;
- to allow for deliveries that are delayed or too small;
- to take advantage of price discounts on large orders;
- to buy items when the price is low and expected to rise;
- to buy items that are going out of production or are difficult to find;
- to make full loads and reduce transport costs;
- to give cover for emergencies.

Management example – stock holdings

Sears plc used to be one of the largest retailers in the UK, owning Selfridges, Miss Selfridge, Freemans (catalogue sales), British Shoe Corporation (Shoe Express, Freeman Hardy Willis, Dolcis, Cable, Hush Puppies, Saxone, Shoe City), Adams, Olympus, Olympus Sportsworld, Millets, Warehouse, Wallis, and Richards. The company has now sold most of its stores and de-merged into separate businesses, but in 1998 the remains of the company reported the following figures:

- Turnover   £1,819 million
- Fixed assets   £743 million
- Number of stores   798
- Stocks   £213 million

Zeneca is a major pharmaceutical business, with a turnover in 1998 of £5.2 billion and an operating profit of £1.1 billion. To support its operations around the world, it has stocks worth £728 million:

- Raw materials and consumables   £197 million
- Work in progress   £216 million
- Finished goods   £315 million

L. T. Francis is a manufacturer of pre-cast concrete fittings for the building trade. Their 1998 annual report gave the following figures:

- Sales £16.4 million
- Total assets £4.3 million
- Stock: raw materials £0.8 million; work in progress £0.4 million; finished goods £2.1 million; total £3.3 million

Sears holds stock of 12 per cent of sales, Zeneca holds 14 per cent, and L. T. Francis 20 per cent. It is not unusual for manufacturers to hold stocks worth more than 25 per cent of annual sales.

Approach of inventory control

The cost of holding stock is typically around 25 per cent of its value a year, so it is not surprising that organizations look for ways of reducing this. It is often thought that minimizing inventory costs is the same as minimizing stocks, but this is not true. If a shop holds no stock at all, it certainly has no inventory costs, but it also has no sales. In practice, the aim is to minimize the sum of the four costs associated with stocks, which are as follows.

- Unit cost: the price charged by the supplier, or the cost of acquiring one unit of the item. It can be fairly easy to find values for this by looking at quotations or recent invoices from suppliers, but it is more difficult when there are several suppliers offering slightly different products or offering different purchase conditions. If a company makes the item itself, it can be difficult to set a reliable transfer price.
- Re-order cost: the cost of placing a repeat order for an item. It might include the cost of administration, receiving, checking goods, and any follow-up. Sometimes the re-order cost includes quality control, transport, sorting and movement of goods received.
- Holding cost: the cost of holding one unit of an item in stock for a unit period of time. It might, for example, be the cost of holding a spare engine in stock for one year. The obvious cost is for tied-up money. This money is either borrowed – in which case interest is paid – or it is cash that the organization could put to another use, in which case there are opportunity costs. Other holding costs are due to storage space, loss, handling, administration and insurance.
- Shortage cost: this occurs when an item is needed but it cannot be supplied from stock. In the simplest case, a retailer may lose direct profit from a sale. However, the effects of shortages are usually much

more widespread and include lost goodwill, loss of reputation, and loss of potential future sales. Shortages of raw materials can disrupt a process and force rescheduling, re-timing of maintenance, and laying off of employees. There may also be costs for expediting orders, sending out emergency orders, paying for special deliveries, storing partly finished goods or using alternative, more expensive suppliers.

Some of these costs – such as the holding cost – will rise with the amount of stock held, while other costs – such as the shortage cost – will fall. Inventory control must balance these competing costs and suggest policies that give the lowest overall costs. To do this, it must answer three basic questions.

1. What items should be stocked? No item, however cheap, should be stocked unless the benefits of stocking it are greater than the costs of doing so. Unfortunately, reliable shortage costs are so difficult to find that this decision is usually a matter of opinion; it relies more on management judgement than on simple calculations.
2. How much should be ordered? If large, infrequent orders are placed, the average stock level is high but the costs of placing and administering orders is low. With small, frequent orders, the average stock level is low but the costs of placing and administering orders is high. The best solution finds an order size that gives a compromise between these two. A standard analysis for this leads to an economic order quantity, which is the best size for orders. This is the basic result of scientific inventory control, and a huge amount of work has been done to modify the models and calculate the best order quantity in many different circumstances.
3. When should an order be placed? This depends on the inventory control system used, type of demand, value of the item, lead time between placing an order and receiving it into stock, supplier reliability, and a number of other factors. These can be included in a re-order level, which is the level the stock is allowed to fall to before it is time to place another order. Essentially, the re-order level sets the amount of stock needed to cover demand in the lead time, and to allow some measure of safety.

Analyses based on the economic order quantity assume that the amount ordered is fixed, and any variation in demand is allowed for by varying the time between orders. The alternative is a periodic review approach.

- Fixed order quantity: this method places an order of fixed size whenever stock falls to the re-order level. A central heating plant, for example, may order 25,000 litres of oil whenever the amount in the tank falls to 2,500 litres. This method requires continuous monitoring of stock levels and is best suited to low, irregular demand for relatively expensive items.

- Periodic review: this method orders varying amounts at regular intervals to raise the amount of stock to a specified level. Supermarket shelves, for example, are refilled every evening to replace whatever has been sold during the day. The operating cost of this system is generally lower and it is better suited to high, regular demand of low-value items.

A huge amount of work has been done on inventory control systems, and there are standard results for most common problems. Although these results are generally easy to find, their interpretation depends to a large extent on management judgement.

Management example – Montague Electrical Engineering

Montague Electrical Engineering (MEE) assembles electric motors, and has annual sales of £8 million. Robert Hellier is the operations manager. In January 1998, he read the monthly inventory report and was surprised to find the total inventory had jumped from £2.2 million in December to £2.6 million.

Hellier noticed the particularly high stocks of part number BCT45, a 3cm diameter bearing costing £5.00. MEE uses around 200 of these a week, and Hellier had been buying 2,500 units at a time, as this seemed a convenient number. When he talked to the accountant, he realized that he had been ordering parts without taking any notice of the inventory costs. His main priority was making sure that there was no disruption to manufacturing, and he had considered the costs of stock as a necessary overhead.

The accountant explained that holding stock cost 30 per cent of its value a year, while it cost about £15 to place an automatic order. The economic order quantity for part number BCT45 was nearer 450 units. This would give an average stock of 300 units, compared with the current policy of 1,300 units, and this alone would save the company £1,500 a year.

MEE had several thousand items in stock, so it was not surprising that the stock levels seemed to be rising out of control. After reviewing the ordering policy for the most widely used items, stocks were reduced to £0.9 million without any reduction in service, saving almost £0.5 million a year.

JOB DESIGN

Most scheduling starts with the simple assumption that each job takes a fixed time. However, it is clear from experience that the time needed to do a job can change – it may be affected by the layout, the equipment available, the physical environment, the motivation of people, the rewards offered, and a whole series of other factors. Organizations obviously want to do each operation in the best possible way, so they must carefully design the way that jobs are done.

> Job design describes the tasks, methods, responsibilities and environment used by individuals to do their work.
> The aim of job design is to find the best possible way of doing a task.

Job design is the most detailed aspect of scheduling. It looks at a range of factors, including decisions about the best order for tasks, who will do the tasks, what skills and equipment they need, how much supervision should be given, how the tasks interact with other operations, and what environment is needed.

Two groups of people are concerned with job design; we will use the usual terms of 'managers' and 'workers'. Job design must satisfy the needs of both of these groups, even though they are completely different. Managers want the workers to be productive so that they meet production, quality and service targets at low costs. On the other hand, the workers' needs are social and psychological – they want to interact with other people, be recognized, appreciated and properly rewarded.

The two main objectives of job design are to meet the productivity, quality and other goals of the organization and to make the job safe, satisfying and rewarding for the individual.

To design jobs that satisfy both of these objectives, three main elements have to be considered:

- the physical environment, where the job is done;
- the social environment, which affects the worker's psychological condition;
- the work methods, which describe how the job is done.

Physical environment

This is the place where the job is done, its layout, the tools used, the equipment available, and so on. If these are badly organized, the environment can be distracting, put heavy burdens on a worker, and even be dangerous. Ergonomics looks at the way the physical environment interacts with the physical capabilities of people, and typically asks questions such as, 'Who will use the workplace?', 'How will the work be done?', 'What must the user see?', 'What must the user hear?', 'Where must the user reach?'

Early studies of the physical environment concentrated on manufacturing machines, but now more emphasis is put on white-collar jobs. The effects of such studies are seen in telephones, which have become lighter and easier to use, with more functions, connecting to computers and other equipment. Other aspects of the work environment relate to the following:

- light – in general, jobs that need higher speed and accuracy need more light;
- temperature and humidity – most people work at their best in temperatures around 18 to 22 degrees;
- noise and vibrations – loud noise is annoying and can damage hearing;
- air pollution – pollution or fumes can be irritating and may be dangerous;
- safety – people must always be given working conditions that are safe, and they must be protected from any possible dangers.

Social environment

The design of a job must also take into account the psychological well-being of the people doing it. An organization must start by preparing employees for their job, and making sure they know exactly what to do. This means giving:

- adequate training for the job;
- adequate supervision and help;
- knowledge of the organization's policies, rules and regulations;
- a clear statement of what is expected from each person;
- credit and rewards for good work.

However, this is only part of the social environment; its wider role is to allow employees to fulfil their needs for self-esteem and personal development. In this way, the social environment offers a higher quality of working life, and this in turn leads to higher motivation and better performance. There are many ways of improving the social environment, including the following:

- allowing people to complete an identifiable and significant part of the process;
- giving meaningful feedback on performance;
- forming coherent teams to work on the process;

- establishing direct relationships with customers, rather than going through supervisors or other intermediaries;
- job rotation – where the job each person does is rotated, so they do not get bored with the same tasks;
- job enlargement – which combines several simple jobs into a larger one;
- job enrichment – which adds more responsibility to the job, and makes it inherently more interesting;
- vertical loading – where people do a range of 'indirect' jobs, such as maintenance, scheduling and administration.

Work methods

Work methods relate to the details of how a task should be done. The usual approach of work methods is to start by looking at the way a job is done at present. Then it breaks the job into a series of small parts and analyses each of these. A hairdresser, for example, will carry out a series of standard tasks – washing hair, cutting with scissors, tidying loose ends, trimming with shears, and so on. Each of these tasks can be broken down into micro-elements, such as reaching out, picking up a hairdryer, and moving the hairdryer back to the customer's head. The micro-elements can be analysed in order to find the most efficient way of doing the whole job. The hairdresser, for example, might spend too long reaching for tools, so the job could be made easier by moving everything nearer to the customer.

In general, work methods ask a series of questions about the job, such as the following:

- Why is this task done?
- What is its purpose?
- How is it done?
- Why is it done this way?
- Could the step be missed out?
- Could it be done at another time?
- Could it be done automatically?
- How could the layout of the workplace be improved?
- Would different tools help?

The answers to these questions may lead to better ways of doing the job.

Management example – Moorhead Stamping Works

Moorhead Stamping Works is a medium-sized company that supplies stamped parts for consumer appliance industries. Their process starts with coils of sheet metal, which are cut into smaller strips using shearing machines. The strips are passed to stamping presses, which form the products. Other processes include welding, painting, plating and assembly.

The working conditions in the plant are far from pleasant. It is noisy, dirty, cluttered, and does not have a good heating and ventilation system. The production planning system has defects, so customer orders are always being expedited, and rushed jobs are common. This puts a lot of pressure on workers. Sometimes, the machines are operated in unsafe conditions and often by poorly trained workers. Government safety and welfare offices are aware of working conditions, and have often sent inspectors to check the plant.

There is poor communication between managers and the workers. Mike Peterson, one of the long-time employees, cannot remember a single occasion when a manager has shown any appreciation of the job done by a worker. On the other hand, he has noticed that managers are always complaining about increased costs and low profits. He is not surprised that the company has high employee turnover, poor quality, declining productivity, and a series of other problems.

CONTROL OF SCHEDULES

Short-term schedules give detailed plans that show what each job, piece of equipment and person should be doing at any time. However, there is a major difference between designing plans and implementing them, so organizations need a control system to monitor progress, report discrepancies with plans, and allow revisions. A control system feeds information back to managers, so they know how operations are going and can take any necessary action (see Figure 7.2). More specifically, the purpose of a control system is to:

- monitor the scheduling to make sure that schedules are designed on time, are accurate and kept up to date;

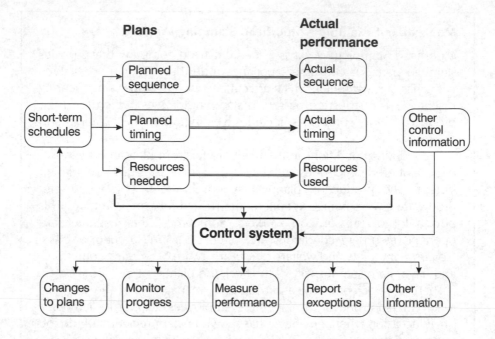

Figure 7.2 *Controlling short-term schedules*

- monitor the operations to make sure that jobs are scheduled according to the plans;
- check that materials, equipment, operators and other resources are available for each job;
- check progress as jobs move through the process;
- report any discrepancies between plans and actual performance;
- warn of problems with progress, delivery dates or available resources;
- allow small adjustments to schedules to overcome minor problems;
- allow complete rescheduling if there are major disruptions to plans;
- assign jobs to specific orders and set delivery times;
- give feedback on times, efficiency, productivity, utilization and other measures of performance.

The inputs for a control system might include a dispatch list (which shows the short-term schedules as an ordered list of the jobs, their importance and how long each will take), inventory records, bills of materials, routing through the machines, and orders for jobs to be done. The main outputs are status and exception reports. Other outputs might include the release of job orders, dispatch of finished jobs and schedule receipts. Such systems can be very complex, need access to large amounts of information and make decisions quickly.

In recent years, there have been changes in the decision-making within some organizations, which have altered this traditional view of control systems. A 'traditional' organization was based on strong managers, whose job was to supervise and control the workers. As times have changed, more emphasis is put on motivating people and encouraging empowered teams to make their own decisions. These teams do not need such formal control, as they effectively take responsibility for their own management. The result is a reduced need for a complicated reporting and control system.

CHAPTER REVIEW

- Short-term schedules give detailed timetables for jobs, people, equipment, raw materials and other resources needed by the process. Designing these schedules is one of the most common problems faced by managers.
- Scheduling jobs on machines is a standard type of problem, which is encountered in many different circumstances. This is a surprisingly difficult problem to solve and the best approaches often use simple rules. There are many more complicated approaches, such as Optimised Production Technology.
- A related problem concerns the scheduling of materials needed by the process. This is generally described as inventory control. Much work has been done analysing different types of inventory systems.
- The aim of inventory control is to minimize the costs of holding stock by answering three basic questions: 'What to stock?', 'When to place orders?', and 'How much to order?'
- The economic order quantity shows the order size that minimizes inventory costs, while the re-order level shows the time to place orders.
- Job design can be viewed as the most detailed level of planning, which looks for the best way of doing a task.
- Three important elements in job design are the physical environment, social environment and work methods.
- A control system is needed to make sure that plans are actually being achieved. This function is increasingly being devolved to empowered teams working on the process.

FURTHER READING

Biemans, F (1990) *Manufacturing Planning and Control*, Elsevier, Amsterdam

Goldratt, E M and Cox, J (1986) *The Goal*, North River Press, New York

Johns, G (1988) *Organizational Behaviour* (2nd edition), Scott, Foresman and Co., Glenview, Il

Landel, R D (1986) *Managing Productivity through People*, Prentice Hall, Englewood Cliffs, NJ

Tersine, R J (1987) *Principles of Inventory and Materials Management* (3rd edition), Elsevier North-Holland, New York

Waters, C D J (1992) *Inventory Control and Management*, John Wiley, Chichester

CHAPTER 8

MRP and JIT

DEPENDENT AND INDEPENDENT DEMAND

Chapters 6 and 7 looked at the planning of resources. This takes forecasts of product demand and uses them to design production plans for the long, medium and short terms. However, sometimes there are better ways of doing this planning; two alternatives are material requirements planning (MRP) and just-in-time systems (JIT) (see Figure 8.1).

Conventional planning is based on forecasts of demand. This assumes that overall demand for a product is made up of individual demands from many separate customers; these demands are independent of each other, so the demand for one product is not related to the demand for another product. However, there are many types of operation in which the demand for one product is not independent, but is clearly related to the demand for another product. This happens when a manufacturer uses a number of

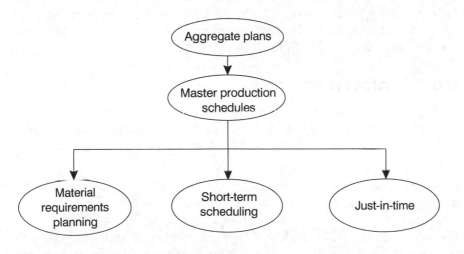

Figure 8.1 *Approaches to short-term scheduling*

components to make a product. The demands for all the components are related, since they depend on the demand for the final product.

Suppose, for example, that a company's master production schedule plans for the assembly of 100 bicycles next week. The company could assume that the demands for wheels and saddles are independent and use projective forecasts based on the historical demand over the past few weeks. However, it would obviously make more sense to assume that the demand for each of these depends on the number of bicycles being assembled. If the company assembles 100 bicycles next week, it will need exactly 200 wheels and 100 saddles. The company can extend this analysis by next looking at the components needed to make 100 wheels, and finding out exactly how many spokes and rims it needs to make sure the wheels are available in time. This is the basis of material requirements planning (MRP).

MATERIAL REQUIREMENTS PLANNING (MRP)

Material requirements planning uses the master production schedule to plan the supply of materials. It 'explodes' the master production schedule to find out the demand for materials, and then schedules these to arrive when they are needed.

The difference in the MRP approaches is illustrated by the way a restaurant chef plans his ingredients for a week's meals. A traditional, independent demand system looks at the ingredients that were used in previous weeks, forecasts demand for next week, and then make sure there is enough of the ingredients in stock to cover this forecast demand. The alternative MRP approach looks at the meals to be cooked each day, uses this schedule to find out exactly what ingredients are needed, and then makes sure these are delivered in time.

The MRP procedure

MRP needs a lot of information about products and does many simple calculations, so it is always computerized. Its main inputs come from three files:

- master production schedule;
- bill of materials; and
- inventory records.

The master production schedule shows the number of units of a product to be made in each period. The bill of materials shows the materials, parts and components needed to make the product, and the order in which they are used. MRP can use the bill of materials to 'explode' the master production schedule and to find out the detailed requirements of materials for each period.

For example, a table is made from a top and four legs, as shown in the bill of materials in Figure 8.2. Each table top is made from a wood kit and hardware, the wood kit is made of four oak planks, and so on. Every product has a bill of materials like this, which is prepared during its design stage.

If the master production schedule shows 10 tables being made in February, there must be 10 tops and 40 legs ready to be assembled at the beginning of February. This gives the gross requirements for parts. However, not all of these will necessarily have to be ordered, as some may already be in stock. Subtracting the current stocks from the gross requirements gives the net requirements for materials.

Now, the quantities to order, and the time when these orders should arrive, are both known. The next step is to find out when to place orders – the lead time before the materials are actually needed. If the table tops and legs have a lead time of 2 weeks, the time to start making them is the middle of January. These parts will then be ready at the end of January just before assembly is due to start. Of course, the orders might need some adjustment to allow for variable lead times, minimum order quantities,

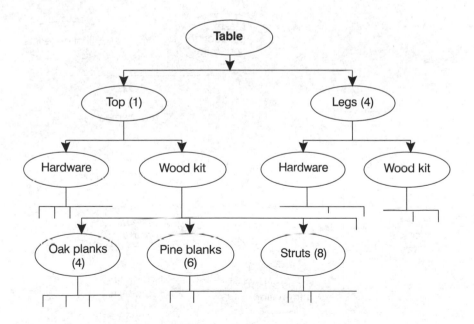

Figure 8.2 *Part of a bill of materials for a table*

discounts, and safety stocks; adding this information gives the detailed timetable for making legs and top. The procedure for this is summarized in Figure 8.3.

This gives the orders for legs and tops, and MRP now uses the same approach to continue down through the rest of the bill of materials. To start making 10 tops in the middle of January, 10 wood kits and 10 hardware packs are needed. If it takes 2 weeks to assemble these, the assembly must be started at the beginning of January. Continuing with this reasoning, it is possible to come up with a timetable for all the materials needed to support the master production schedule. The MRP system will also give exception reports, performance reviews, inventory records, and a range of other information, as shown in Figure 8.4.

Benefits of MRP

Independent demand inventory systems use forecasts to find likely demand, and then hold stocks that are high enough to meet these. However, forecasts will always contain errors; to allow for these, organizations using traditional systems hold more stocks than they really need. MRP avoids the cost of these extra stocks by relating the supply of materials directly to demand. Other benefits of MRP include the following:

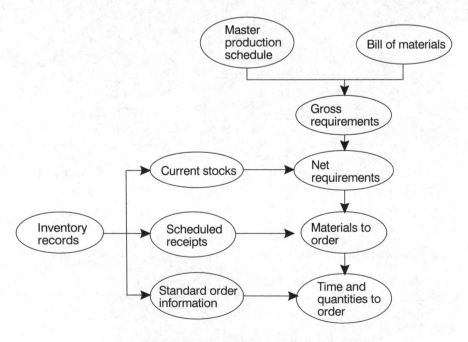

Figure 8.3 *The MRP procedure*

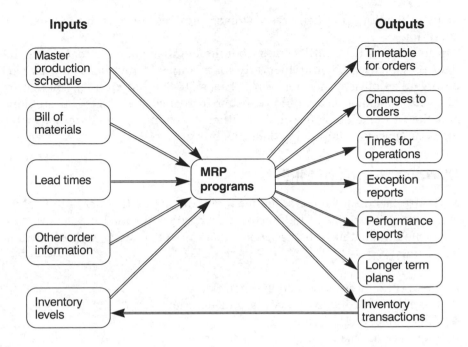

Figure 8.4 *Inputs and outputs from an MRP system*

- materials supply is linked directly to known demand;
- stock levels are lower, with savings in capital, space, warehousing, and so on;
- there is a higher stock turnover;
- customer service is better, with no delays due to shortages of materials;
- delivery times are more reliable and faster;
- there is a higher utilization of facilities, as materials are always available when needed;
- less time is spent on expediting and emergency orders;
- better planning is encouraged;
- MRP schedules can be used for short-term planning;
- MRP shows the priority of jobs supplying materials.

As the analyses of MRP are based completely on a master production schedule, organizations are more likely to design a reliable plan and stick to it. This gives better overall planning. The MRP analyses can also give early warning of problems and shortages, so that expediting can speed up deliveries, or production plans can be changed. In this way, MRP improves the wider performance of the organization, measured in terms of equipment utilization, productivity, customer service, and response to market conditions.

Another benefit of MRP comes from the detailed analyses that can highlight previously hidden problems. If, for example, a supplier is unreliable, an organization may not notice if it keeps stocks that are high enough to hide the inadequacy. It would be better to realize that there is a problem and then to take steps to solve it, either by changing the supplier or by discussing ways of improving their reliability.

Disadvantages of MRP

MRP also has disadvantages, the most obvious being the amount of information that it requires. The process starts with a detailed master production schedule that must be designed some time in advance, so MRP cannot be used if:

- there is no master production schedule;
- the master production schedule is inaccurate;
- plans are changed frequently;
- plans are not made far enough in advance.

MRP also needs details of the bill of materials, information about current stocks, orders outstanding, lead times, and other information about suppliers. Many organizations simply do not have this information. Other organizations have data that does not have enough detail, or the right format, or enough accuracy. Even when all the information is available, the complexity of MRP systems can lead to difficulties. There is a huge amount of data manipulation, so MRP can only be used when all related systems are computerized and integrated.

Apart from the limited circumstances in which it can be used, and the amount of data manipulation required, there are other problems with MRP. It might, for example, reduce flexibility in responding to changes. With MRP, the only materials available are those needed for the specified master production schedule; this plan cannot be changed at short notice as the materials needed for any other plan will not be available. The disadvantages of MRP may be summarized as follows:

- it requires a large amount of detailed and reliable information;
- it uses a lot of data manipulation;
- systems can be very complex;
- it reduces flexibility;
- it assumes that lead times are constant and independent of the quantities ordered;

- in practice, materials are made in a different order to that specified in the bill of materials;
- if MRP is used to schedule the production of parts, this may give poor schedules;
- it may not recognize capacity and other constraints;
- it can be expensive and time-consuming to implement.

Management example – Alco Office Supplies

Alco Office Supplies makes a range of desks, filing cabinets and other office furniture. In 1997, the company started using MRP for its standard filing cabinets. The manufacturing process was simple, and, with the help of a consultant, a new system was working in slightly less than a year at a cost of £95,000. By the end of the second year of operation, the system was judged a success and was extended to other products.

Alco's move to MRP illustrates how much information is needed. Although it had integrated computer systems, these had to be thoroughly checked and overhauled before they were reliable enough for MRP. The biggest single job was to obtain data in a suitable form. Some of the old systems updated data records overnight, and these had to be replaced with real-time systems, with all data consolidated into a company-wide database.

Alco's experience also shows the complexity of real MRP systems. Its standard four-drawer filing cabinet is assembled from 218 different parts. Many of these are small and duplicated, but exploding the master production schedule requires a lot of calculations. The company makes 24 variations on this basic filing cabinet, and a total of 3,500 different products. Each of these needs a separate MRP run, and then common parts are combined into larger orders.

On Alco's first trial run of the MRP system, the weekly report was over 8,000 pages long. Needless to say, when the system became operational, this was trimmed – to 200 pages.

Extensions to MRP

MRP only became feasible in the 1970s, with the development of cheap computing. The first users came from manufacturing industries, but service industries quickly began to see that they could use the same approach to schedule materials, labour, and other resources.

- Hospitals use MRP to schedule surgical operations and make sure that supplies and equipment are ready when needed. The schedules of surgery gives the planned operations in any period, the 'bill of material' contains information about the equipment and resources needed for each type of surgery, and the inventory file contains information about surgical instruments, disposable materials, reusable instruments, sterilized materials, and so on.
- Restaurants use MRP to schedule food and equipment. Menus give the meals planned for the restaurant, and the recipes for each meal provide the bill of materials.
- Universities' master production schedules show the number of students who will be graduating from each programme in each term. The bill of materials describes the courses the students take in each term. Then MRP can find the number of teachers, classrooms, laboratories, and so on.

MRP has proved so successful that the basic system has been extended in several ways. Early extensions to MRP added feedback, in order to help with planning decisions. There are two important types of feedback:

- if proposed plans would break some capacity constraints, this is detected by MRP and early rescheduling is done. This means that MRP can take an active part in capacity planning;
- if actual performance is interrupted, the master production schedule can be revised quickly with inputs from the MRP system.

The next major extension to MRP is manufacturing resource planning, or MRP II.

Organizations soon began to realize that the MRP approach of exploding a master production schedule to find material needs could be extended to other functions. Ordering and purchasing were included in MRP, but it was felt that the analyses might be extended to dispatching, distribution, production processes and even marketing and finance. A master production schedule can show the amount of machinery and equipment needed in each period. This, in turn, will set levels for manning and other resources. Eventually, the master production schedule can form the basis for planning most of the resources used in a process. This is the aim of MRP II. In principle, it can relate all planning and control decisions to the master production schedule. In practice, however, it is very difficult to implement such complicated and comprehensive systems. The result is that many organizations work with partial MRP II, which links together parts of the process and gives schedules for some resources.

MRP and its extensions give a very useful approach to scheduling. However, the different approaches do have their disadvantages, and many organizations find it very difficult to cope with the complexity of working systems. Many have looked for simpler approaches, which would give the benefits of MRP, but with less effort. One very important development in this area is just-in-time operations.

JUST-IN-TIME OPERATIONS (JIT)

Just-in-time (JIT) organizes all operations so that they occur just at the time when they are needed. This means, for example, that if materials are needed for production, they are not bought some time in advance and kept in stock, but are delivered directly to the production process just as they are needed. If materials arrive just as they are needed, stocks of work in progress can be eliminated.

JIT is not a new idea. In the 1920s, iron ore arriving at the Ford plant in Detroit was turned into steel within a day, and into finished cars a few days later. This was a very efficient way of using resources and reducing stocks of work in progress, but few organizations at the time followed Ford's example. Even today, most organizations feel compelled to hold large stocks, to ensure smooth operations and to safeguard against disruptions to the process. The view that inventories are essential makes managers ask the question, 'How can we provide stocks at lowest cost?' However, during the past few years, some organizations have changed their view and have started to ask another question: 'How can we eliminate stocks?' The answer to this has laid the foundations of JIT.

One way to start describing JIT is by looking at its effect on inventories (although it must be remembered that this is just one aspect of just-in-time operations). The main reason for holding stock is to allow for short-term mismatches between supply and demand. Most organizations allow for this mismatch by keeping stocks that are high enough to cover any expected demand. Sometimes, particularly with widely varying demand, doing this requires very high stock levels. MRP overcomes this problem by using the master schedule to match the supply of materials more closely to demand. The more closely the supply is matched to demand, the smaller the stocks that are needed in order to cover any differences. If the mismatch can be completely eliminated, so can stocks; at this point, just-in-time operations will be in place.

JIT can be illustrated by the image of a car assembly line. As the chassis moves down the line to a work station, an engine arrives at the same point and is fitted. This is repeated for all other parts; as the car body arrives at another work station, four doors also arrive and are added. All the way down the line, materials arrive just at the time when they are needed, so the car is assembled in one smooth process.

JIT is a simple idea, and its argument about inventories can be summarized as follows:

- Stocks are held in an organization to cover short-term variation and uncertainty in supply and demand.
- JIT assumes that these stocks serve no useful purpose; they only exist because poor co-ordination fails to match the supply of materials to the demand.
- As long as stocks are held, managers will not try to improve their co-ordination.
- This means that operations will continue to be poorly managed, with many problems hidden by the holding of stocks.
- The proper move for an organization is to improve its management, find the reasons why there are differences between supply and demand, and then take whatever action is needed to overcome those differences.

This reasoning leads to a wide view of JIT. Although it has been introduced as a way of reducing stock levels, it is much more than this and really involves a change in the way an organization looks at its operations. Its supporters describe it as 'a way of eliminating waste', or 'a way of enforcing problem-solving'.

JIT sees an organization as having a series of problems that hinder efficient operations. These problems include long equipment set-up times, unbalanced operations, constrained capacity, machine breakdowns, defective materials, interrupted operations, unreliable suppliers, poor quality, too much paperwork and too many changes. Stock is held to avoid the effects of these problems and, effectively, it hides them from sight. A much more constructive approach is to identify the problems, and solve them. This approach leads to a number of changes in viewpoint.

- Stocks – organizations hold stocks to cover short-term differences between supply and demand. JIT assumes that these stocks hide problems, and suggests that organizations should identify the reasons why there are differences between supply and demand, and then take whatever action is needed to remove them.

■ Quality – JIT can only work if materials are delivered with perfect quality, so total quality management (see Chapter 9) is essential.

■ Suppliers – many people feel that suppliers and customers are in some sort of conflict, where one can only benefit at the expense of the other. JIT relies totally on its suppliers, so it cannot allow this kind of friction. Instead, it sees customers and suppliers as partners with a common objective – a mutually beneficial trading arrangement. This works best when an organization finds a single supplier who can meet their conditions, and a long-term relationship is developed. At one time after introducing JIT, Toyota was using 250 suppliers, while General Motors, which had not yet introduced JIT, was using 4,000.

■ Reliability – when equipment breaks down, most organizations start to work on another process or another product. JIT does not allow this flexibility, so it forces managers to recognize that there is a problem with reliability, and to take whatever actions are needed to make sure the equipment does not break down.

■ Employees – in some organizations, there is friction between 'managers' and 'workers'. This is largely caused by systems that reward managers for the profits of the company, and see workers as costs that drain the profits. JIT recognizes that all employees should be concerned with, and rewarded for, the success of their organization, and that they should all be treated fairly and equitably.

■ Responsibilities – in return for their fair treatment, JIT demands more from employees. They are given authority to stop a process and solve any problem that is causing a disruption, so some responsibility moves from managers working at a distance, to people working directly on the process. JIT also needs people to be flexible enough to do a variety of jobs, adapt to new practices, possess relevant skills and knowledge, participate actively in the running of the organization, and be interested in its success.

■ Simple operations – JIT always emphasizes simplicity in many ways – it recommends replacing large, complicated equipment with smaller pieces that are easier to control; moving management decisions closer to the work; avoiding planning by remote computer systems; using a process layout to give a smooth flow of products; and simplifying product designs.

Management example – just-in-time at Guy La Rochelle International

Guy La Rochelle International is one of Europe's leading manufacturers of cosmetics and toiletries. One of its main problems is that customers' tastes change very quickly, and it has to react by making rapid changes to products.

La Rochelle has a production plant near Lyon that employs 900 people. Over time, the process has evolved and it now uses just-in-time manufacturing. At the same time, the changing demands require flexible operations that are based on small batches and short production runs. With JIT, the length of production runs has declined from an average of 2 days to 3 hours, and the equipment set-up times have been reduced to a minimum. The result is smaller batch sizes, less inventory, better service, a fast response to changing customers' tastes, and guarantees that customers never get stale products that have been sitting on a shelf.

The inventory-holding cost is 25 per cent, so, when La Rochelle reduced its stock of lipstick by $1 million, it saved $250,000 a year. Their Baby Soft bath oil has changed from a production run of 60,000 units every 30 days, to 10,000 units every 5 days; the run of 200,000 units of lipstick every 65 days has changed to 60,000 units every 20 days.

The conversion to JIT is well supported and liked by La Rochelle employees. Every worker now has a more varied job, a range of new skills, better rewards, and they enjoy working in teams rather than as individuals.

When can JIT be used?

JIT can only be used in certain types of organization. It is particularly suited to large-scale production that makes identical products in a continuous process. It is not surprising, therefore, that one of the most successful users of JIT is the car assembly plant. There are clearly a number of conditions that must be met before an organization can consider JIT:

- Every time production is changed from one item to another there are delays, disruptions and costs. According to JIT, these changes waste resources and should be eliminated. JIT requires a stable environment that makes a single product – or limited variations on a standard product – at a fixed level over some time.
- A stable environment allows specialized equipment to be used. The fixed costs of this equipment can best be recovered through high production volumes, so JIT works best with high-volume, mass production operations.
- The specified production level must give a smooth flow of products through the process. If each part of the process is to have high utilization, careful planning is needed to make sure the work flow is balanced.

- Deliveries of materials are made just at the time when they are needed. It is usually impractical to bring individual units from suppliers, so the next best thing is to use very small batches. Suppliers must adapt to this kind of operation.
- If small batches are used, re-order costs must be reduced as much as possible, otherwise the frequent deliveries will be too expensive. A common approach to this uses flexible manufacturing.
- Lead times must be short, otherwise the delay in answering a request for materials is too long. This requires close work with suppliers, perhaps including having them build facilities that are physically close.
- When materials arrive just as they are needed, there are no stocks to give safety cover. Any defects will disrupt operations, so suppliers must be totally reliable and provide materials that are always free from defects.
- If something goes wrong and there is a disruption to the process, the workforce must be able to find the cause of the problem, correct the fault, and make sure that it does not happen again. This requires a skilled and flexible workforce that is committed to the success of the organization.

Continuing the argument in this way, it is possible to list the key elements in JIT operations, which include:

- a stable environment;
- standard products with few variations;
- continuous production at fixed levels;
- automated, high-volume operations;
- a balanced process that fully uses resources;
- reliable production equipment;
- minimum stocks;
- small batches of materials;
- short lead times for materials;
- low set-up and delivery costs;
- efficient materials handling;
- reliable suppliers;
- consistently high quality of materials;
- flexible workforce;
- fair treatment and rewards for employees;
- ability to solve any problems; and
- an efficient method of control.

Management example – Japanese motorcycles

In the 1960s, domestic demand for motorcycles in many countries was satisfied by local manufacturers. These included Harley-Davidson in the USA, BSA in Britain and BMW in Germany. After dramatic changes in the industry, many well-established companies went out of business. Their problem was the new competition from the Japanese companies of Honda, Yamaha, Suzuki and Kawasaki.

These four companies could supply motorcycles anywhere in the world, with a higher quality and a lower cost than competitors. In 1978, Harley-Davidson (H-D) in the USA tried to prove that the Japanese companies were dumping motorcycles on the market at less than the cost of manufacture. This attempt failed, as evidence given at the hearings showed that the Japanese companies had operating costs that were 30 per cent lower than Harley-Davidson's. One of the main reasons for this was their use of JIT manufacturing.

By the mid-1980s, H-D was on the edge of bankruptcy, as its share of the US heavyweight motorcycle market fell to 20 per cent. It recognized that it could only compete by using the same methods as its competitors, and adopted JIT in 1982. Despite initial problems, H-D stuck to its 'materials as needed' programme, and is now succeeding once again in a very competitive market. In a 5-year period, machine set-up times were reduced by 75 per cent, warranty and scrap costs by 60 per cent, and work-in-progress stocks by $22 million. During the same period, productivity rose by 30 per cent. Sales rose to new records, but were limited to 60 per cent of the market by a shortage of capacity, so the company spent $275 million on expansions.

Achieving just-in-time operations

In its efforts to reduce waste, JIT views administration as an overhead that is largely wasted. It tries to simplify operations and minimize the effort needed to control them. This means that JIT control systems are usually manual, with little paperwork, and most decisions are made at the actual operations. This is in marked contrast to MRP systems, which are computerized, expensive to run, and have decisions made by planners who are some distance away.

This aim of simplicity means that the methods used by JIT are all practical and based largely on common sense. Process layouts are simplified and made more efficient; product designs are simplified so they are easier to make; set-up procedures are changed to make them faster; re-order costs are reduced to allow smaller deliveries; suppliers are encouraged to make small deliveries; everyone in the organization is trained in quality management; and routine maintenance of equipment is scheduled to avoid breakdowns. These, and the other elements of JIT, all seem very simple, but they have a major effect on the operations. These effects are so important that they cannot be introduced in one go, but evolve with small continuous improvements over a long time. Toyota, for example, made continuous improvements in its operations for 25 years before it adopted a reasonable JIT system.

This shows one reason why there is often misunderstanding about JIT. It is based on simple ideas, but these simple ideas are very difficult to implement. Carrying out operations just as they are needed seems an obvious and simple way of organizing work, but it can be very difficult to get a whole process to work efficiently in this way.

The usual way of co-ordinating JIT process is to use 'kanbans' – Japanese for 'card' – or visible record. All operations are controlled by kanbans, which 'pull' materials through a process; with MRP and other systems, materials are 'pushed' through the process. The difference in these approaches can be seen in the way reports are handled in Westshires Market Analysis. In a 'push' system, such as MRP, every stage in the process has its own short-term schedule that is designed to meet the master production schedule. Jane in Westshires may have a timetable that says she must analyse ten reports on Monday morning. She takes these from her in-tray, and, when she is finished, she passes them to Bill's in-tray. Bill's timetable says that he has to work on these ten reports on Tuesday morning. The major drawback with this approach is that every stage in the process is essentially working in isolation. If Bill has a problem and is delayed, Jane still works according to her schedule, leading to a build-up in Bill's in-tray. On the other hand, if Bill finishes early, he has to sit and wait idly until Jane passes him the reports.

Each operation in this sort of 'push' system is distinct, and not linked to other parts of the process. As soon as one stage finishes its work, it pushes the results through to the next stage, regardless of what the next stage is doing.

An alternative 'pull' system – like JIT – links the different operations, by sending messages backwards down the process asking for a delivery of materials. So Jane and Bill, instead of working to separate schedules, have their work linked through an overall delivery schedule. Bill receives a message to say that the person after him will soon be ready for the next report, so he finishes work on this report and passes it on, while sending a message back to Jane that he is ready to start work on the next report. The result is that work is pulled rather than pushed through the process, and is only passed on when it is actually needed.

Kanbans give a way of co-ordinating such 'pull' systems. There are several ways of using kanbans. The simplest is illustrated in Figure 8.5 and set out below as follows:

- All material is stored and moved in standard containers, with different sizes of container for each material. A container can only be moved when it has a kanban attached to it.
- When an operation needs more materials – when its stock of materials falls to a re-order level – a kanban is attached to an empty container and this is taken to the preceding operation. The kanban is then attached to a full container, which is returned to the operation.
- The empty container is a signal for the preceding operation to start work on this material, and just enough is produced to refill the container.

It is clear that the main features of this single kanban system are as follows.

- A message is passed backwards to the preceding operation to start production, and it only makes enough to fill a container.
- Standard containers are used, which hold a specific amount. This amount is usually quite small, typically 10 per cent of a day's needs.
- The size of each container is the smallest reasonable batch that can be made, and there are usually only one or two full containers at any point.

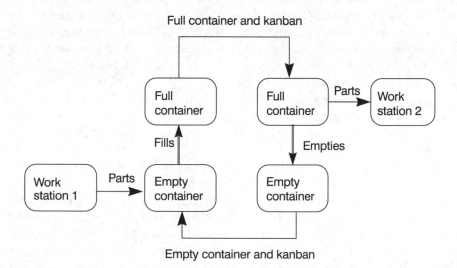

Figure 8.5 *Simplest form of kanban system*

- A specific number of containers and/or kanbans is used.
- The stock of work in progress can be controlled by limiting the size of containers and the number of kanbans.
- Materials can only be moved in containers, and containers can only be moved when they have a kanban attached. This gives a rigid means of controlling the amount of materials produced and the time when they are moved.
- While it is simple to administer, this system makes sure that work-in-progress stocks cannot accumulate.

Benefits and disadvantages of JIT

JIT can lead to a dramatic reduction of stocks of raw materials and work in progress. Some organizations have reduced these by more than 75 per cent. This gives a number of other benefits, such as reductions in space needed, lower warehousing costs, less investment in stocks, and so on. Other benefits of JIT come from the reorganization needed to achieve a working system. Several of these have already been mentioned, including:

- lower stocks of raw materials and work in progress;
- reduced lead times;
- shorter time needed to make a product;
- higher productivity;
- higher equipment utilization;
- simplified planning and scheduling;
- less paperwork;
- improved quality of materials and products;
- less scrap and wastage;
- better morale in the workforce;
- better relations with suppliers;
- emphasis on solving problems in the process.

Some of these benefits can only be bought at a high price. Making high-quality products with few interruptions caused by breakdowns, for example, usually means that better equipment must be used. Reduced set-up times usually require more sophisticated equipment. This equipment must respond quickly to changing demands, so there must be more capacity. Therefore, JIT can only work if organizations buy better, more flexible equipment with higher capacity. Many smaller organizations have found that this costs too much, particularly if the cost of training all employees is added. Although the long-term rewards may be high, the short-term costs of JIT can be prohibitive for many organizations.

There are some disadvantages with JIT, apart from the fact that it may be expensive to implement, and involve many years of slow progress. Its inflexibility is another weakness. It makes it difficult to change product design, mix or demand levels, so it does not work well with irregular demand, small production numbers, specially ordered material, or strongly seasonal demand.

Some of the benefits of JIT may also be seen as disadvantages. Having frequent set-ups and small batches, for example, is essential for JIT, but unless an organization is careful, this can give high re-order costs. Similarly, JIT needs decisions to be made close to operations, and such devolved decision-making – with responsibility given to lower levels in the workforce – may be an advantage or a disadvantage depending on the company's viewpoint.

The specific problems identified by JIT users can be summarized as follows:

- initial investment and cost of implementation;
- time needed to achieve improvements;
- reliance on perfect quality of materials from suppliers;
- problems with maintaining product quality;
- inability of suppliers to adapt to JIT methods;
- need for stable production when demands from customers may vary;
- customers demanding a wide range of options with products;
- reduction in flexibility to change products;
- difficulty of reducing set-up times;
- lack of commitment within the organization;
- lack of co-operation and trust between employees;
- problems linking to existing information systems;
- need to change layout of facilities;
- increased stress in the workforce.

CHAPTER REVIEW

- Material requirements planning (MRP) is an example of dependent demand planning. It 'explodes' the master production schedule, using a bill of materials, to give timetables for the supply of materials and other operations.
- MRP needs a lot of information and data manipulation before it can be used. Originally, this limited its use to large manufacturers, but the approach is now used in many different kinds of organization.
- The main benefit of MRP is its ability to match the supply of materials to known demands. This reduces stock levels and associated costs.

- There are several extensions to the basic MRP, notably MRP II.
- Just-in-time systems aim to eliminate waste from an organization by having operations occur just as they are needed. This approach is deceptively simple, but needs a new way of thinking based on solving problems rather than hiding them.
- JIT changes an organization's view of operations, giving different attitudes towards inventories, quality, lead times, suppliers, employees and many other factors.
- JIT can only be used in certain types of organization. In particular, it needs a stable environment, small batches, short lead times, and total quality management.
- JIT needs a simple control system, which is provided by kanbans.

FURTHER READING

Cheng, T C E and Podolsky, S (1996) *Just in Time Manufacturing* (2nd edition), Chapman and Hall, London

Hutchins, D (1989) *Just in Time*, Gower Press, London

Luscombe, M (1993) *MRP II: Integrating the Business*, Butterworth-Heinemann, London

Schniederjans, M J (1993) *Topics in Just-in-Time Management*, Allyn and Bacon, Boston

Waters, C D J (1992) *Inventory Control and Management*, John Wiley, Chichester

CHAPTER 9

Quality Management

DEFINITIONS OF QUALITY

With just-in-time systems, materials arrive at operations just as they are needed. As no safety stocks are held, the materials delivered must be of perfect quality. In the past, people believed that it was impossible to achieve this perfect quality, and that some faults were inevitable. Now this is known to be false, and quality management can make sure that an organization's products are always good enough to satisfy customer demand.

Organizations now pay a lot of attention to the quality of their products. Ford uses the slogan, 'Quality is Job 1'; IBM says, 'We will deliver defect-free competitive products and services on time to our customers'; Vauxhall says that 'Quality is a right, not a privilege'; thousands of companies advertise that they are 'ISO 9000 registered for quality', and the main objective of many of them is to make 'products of the highest quality'. What exactly do they mean by 'quality', and how can they make products without any defects?

MEASURING QUALITY

The first problem is to give a reasonable definition of 'quality'. For example, it is possible to say whether or not you enjoyed reading a novel, but it is difficult to give an objective measure of its quality. If a survey asks for an opinion of the government, it might be possible to talk about its various policies, but difficult to give a convincing description of its overall quality. It is often difficult to give a simple measure of product quality, but some useful observations are possible. For example, a ball-point pen is seen to be of good quality if it writes easily and clearly; an airline is deemed to have given a high-quality service if the passengers arrive at their destination on time and without too much hassle; an electricity supplier gives a high-quality service if the customer never has to worry about supplies or costs.

In other words, a product is considered to be of high quality if it does the job for which it was designed. This gives one view of quality, based on a product's ability to meet customer expectations.

In its broadest sense, quality is the ability of a product to meet – and, preferably, exceed – customer expectations.
Quality management is concerned with all aspects of a product's quality.

Unfortunately, this still gives a rather vague idea of 'quality', especially as different customers have different expectations. The problem is that quality depends on many factors. For example, the quality of a television set may be judged by how expensive it is, how attractive the cabinet is, its size, how easy it is to operate, the clarity of the picture, the colours, what format it uses, how often it needs repairing, how long it will last, the number of channels it can pick up, how good the sound is, what additional features it has, and so on. The quality of almost any product can be judged using similar criteria, perhaps including the following:

- innate excellence;
- fitness for intended use;
- performance;
- reliability;
- durability;
- specific features, perhaps for safety or convenience;
- technology used;
- conformance to design specifications;
- uniformity, with small variability;
- perception of high quality by customers;
- convenience of use;
- attractive appearance and style;
- ratio of performance to cost;
- customer service before and during sales;
- on-time deliveries;
- after-sales service.

A reasonable view of quality must take into account many such factors, and a product should not be judged by some factors while others are ignored. For example, a doctor's quality cannot be judged by counting the number of patients seen without considering the treatment given; nor can a computer be judged simply by its performance without taking into account how long it will last; a government's quality cannot be judged by its defence policy alone, ignoring its handling of the economy. Organizations must consider a combination of factors, which, taken together, will define high quality.

Some of these factors can be measured, such as weight, number of break-downs a year and guaranteed life. It is fairly easy to design specifications for the quality of these factors, and then to test the products to make sure they are achieving the standards. Other factors cannot be measured, but rely on judgement; these include appearance, comfort and courtesy of staff. These subjective factors are much more difficult to assess and monitor. This is a particular problem with services, where the quality is judged largely by customer opinion; it is not possible, for example, to measure the quality of a haircut, but most people know when they get a bad one. Typically, the quality of a service is judged by the following:

- reliability;
- availability;
- credibility;
- security;
- competence of staff;
- understanding of customer needs;
- responsiveness to customers;
- courtesy of staff;
- comfort of surroundings;
- communication between participants; and
- associated goods provided with the service

How can an organization identify whether it is meeting customer expectations in these areas? The usual way is to give customers a questionnaire after they receive the service, and ask them to give scores for different features. The response to these questionnaires shows how closely customer expectations are being met, and which areas need improvement.

Management example – Grand & Toy

Grand & Toy (G&T) was founded in 1882 and now has 70 shops selling office supplies, business furniture and printed forms. They provide a service package that has four parts – goods supplied, facilities, explicit services and implicit services. G & T judges the quality of its service by its performance in these four areas.

Goods – which are bought by customers. G&T stocks more than 3,000 different items in each shop, but 10,000 items are kept in central stores and can be delivered very quickly. The company only keeps high-quality goods in stock, and low-quality or damaged goods are immediately discarded. If a customer wants something that is not available, the staff will trace the product and arrange its delivery as soon as possible.

Facilities – the shops and warehouses. The shops are conveniently located in city centres, often within shopping malls. They are well designed and laid out in a standard pattern with no annoying lights, sights or noises. To attract customers' attention, three display units are put at the front with special offers, and all shelves are obviously well stocked. The shops are clean, well carpeted, attractive, and welcoming, with staff continually cleaning the shop during quiet periods.

Explicit services – these are benefits that are readily observable and define the essential features of the service. G&T believes that its staff are the most important part of its service package. All staff have on-the-job training, weekly meetings to discuss products, concerns and plans, and are encouraged to study product development and sales techniques. G&T aims for a consistent service across its shops, and part of the training describes the service that staff must give to customers. This goes beyond selling, and includes giving information and advice. Staff times are scheduled so that no customer has to wait long for service, even at busy times.

Implicit services – these are benefits that are not readily observable but that enhance the customer's experience. G&T attracts the best employees by offering competitive wages, benefits, opportunities for promotion and an attractive workplace. Because of the good working conditions, the staff are friendly to customers, proud of their company and enthusiastic about their job. Surveys have found a very high level of customer satisfaction with the staff and shops in general.

QUALITY CONTROL

The traditional way of maintaining the quality of a product is to use quality control

Quality control uses a series of inspections and tests to check that planned quality is actually achieved.

Quality control takes a sample of units and makes sure that their performance in key areas is within acceptable limits – for example, that the weight of breakfast cereal in a packet is within a specified range, or that the number of trains arriving on time reaches an agreed level. Quality control generally takes a random sample of units and tests these to see how many meet designed specifications. If a pre-determined number of units of the sample reaches the designed standard, the product is said to be of acceptable quality; if fewer than the pre-determined number reach the designed standard, the product's quality is not acceptable and some remedial action must be taken.

This approach raises a series of questions: How often should the tests be done? Where should they be done? What is the best sample size? What defines acceptable performance? How many must achieve this standard? The answers to these questions come from the well-tested analyses of statistical quality control, but another obvious question is, 'Why use a sample and not test every unit?' There are several answers to this, including the following:

- Expense – it may be too expensive to test every unit, particularly if the number of defects is small.
- Time needed – some tests are so long or complicated that they cannot be fitted into normal operations.
- Destructive tests – sometimes, tests are destructive. A factory making light bulbs could find out their average life by testing all the production, but then there would be no bulbs left to sell.
- Reliability – testing all units may be no more reliable than testing a sample. No inspection is completely reliable, as there are random variations, inspectors become tired or bored, people make mistakes, automatic tests develop faults, and subjective judgements are needed.
- Feasibility – in some cases, an infinite number of tests could be done. To test the effectiveness of a medicine completely, it must be given to everybody who might take it, in all possible circumstances. This gives an almost infinite number of possible tests.

In practice, these arguments in favour of samples rather than complete tests have become less convincing in recent years. Organizations now recognize that random inspections do not guarantee high quality, and have adopted a more rigorous approach.

Quality control inspections

There are basically two types of inspection in statistical quality control:

- 'acceptance sampling' tests the quality of products. It is done at the end of an operation to see whether batches of the products should be accepted or rejected, and is primarily concerned with the detection of defects;
- 'process control' tests the performance of the process. It is done during operations to see if the process is working within acceptable limits or if it needs adjusting. This is primarily concerned with the prevention of faults.

Both of these types of inspection work with random samples of products, and they both suffer from the problem that such tests can never be completely reliable. There is always some variation in the output of a process, which is why organizations define 'acceptable quality' as performing within specified limits. Provided a bar of chocolate weighs between, say, 249.9g and 250.1g, most people do not mind that it does not weigh exactly the advertised 250g. However, products should be as close to the specified quality as possible as people would certainly not be impressed if the weight of their bars of chocolate varied by 50g, or even 10g. All operations should aim to reduce variability, and both the product and the process must be designed to allow for small variations and still give products of reliably high quality.

If there is less variation in the final product, most units will be close to the specifications. However, occasionally, even with a reliable process, the performance will go outside acceptable limits and the product thus becomes defective. When this happens, it is clearly a sign that something has gone wrong. Faults are typically caused by:

- human errors in the operations;
- faults in equipment;
- defects in raw materials;
- faults in operations, such as speed or temperature changes;
- changes in the environment, such as humidity, dust or temperature; and
- errors in monitoring equipment, such as faults in measuring tools.

Unfortunately, sampling alone will not detect all such defects. Suppose that a batch of 100 units actually has 10 defective units. In a sample of 10 units from the batch, one defect may be found, but there are random variations, and, in the extremes, a sample might show either 10 defects, or none. Any test using a sample might reject a good batch because the particular sample has an unexpectedly large number of defects, or it might accept a bad batch because the particular sample has an unexpectedly small number of defects.

Another problem with inspections is that they are generally carried out at the later stages of the process, often just before the finished products are delivered to customers. This might seem sensible, as there is more chance of a product being faulty by the end of the process, so all defects can be found in one big inspection at the end. However, the longer a unit is in a process, the more time and money is spent on it. It really makes more sense to find any faults as early as possible, before any more money is wasted by working on a defective unit. The best option for a baker, for example, is to detect bad eggs when they arrive at the bakery, rather than use the eggs and then scrap the finished cakes (see Figure 9.1).

The major effort in quality control should be expended at the beginning of the process, or even earlier. It should start with routine tests of materials sent by suppliers, and there is a strong case for inspections to start within suppliers' own operations. Inspections should then continue all the way from the production of raw materials through to the completion of the final product and its delivery to customers. Some particularly important places for inspections are:

- for raw materials – both during material suppliers' operations; and on arrival at the organization;
- during the process – at regular intervals during the process; before high-cost operations; before irreversible operations, such as firing pottery; before operations that might hide defects, such as painting;
- for finished products – when production is complete; and before shipping to customers.

If the main effort of inspection is made early enough, very few defects should be found at later stages of the process By the time the product gets to the customer it should be as free from defects as possible.

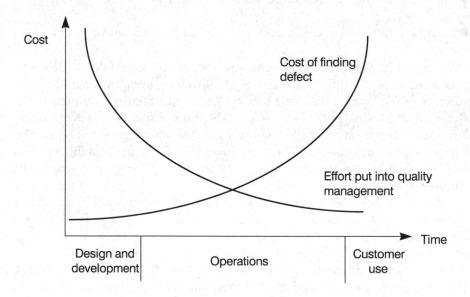

Figure 9.1 *Cost of finding a defect and quality management effort*

Management example – Stroh Brewery Company

The Stroh Brewery Company of Detroit is a major producer of American beer. One of their plants is the Winston-Salem brewery, which occupies over 100,000 square metres and makes 200 million gallons of canned beer a year.

Quality control of beer is rigorous and includes 1,100 tests on each batch of beer. The brewery checks everything from taste to the quantity in each can, with 38 testers employed in three separate laboratories for microbiology, brewing and packaging. If problems are found, the quality control department can stop production at any point and investigate them.

A typical test in the brewing laboratory checks the number of yeast cells during fermentation. Beer must have a standard 16 million yeast cells (± 2 million) per millilitre of beer. For this test, a small sample of beer is taken during fermentation, diluted and the cells are counted through a microscope.

A typical test in the packaging laboratory checks the amount of air in a beer can. Because air can affect the taste, the company allows a maximum of 1cc of air in a can. This is checked by testing 3 cans from the production line 5 times per shift. If a sample is found with more than 1cc of air, the entire batch is put 'in quarantine' and systematically tested to find the point at which the canning has gone wrong. As each line fills 1,600 cans a minute, this can lead to a lot of testing.

COSTS OF QUALITY

In recent years, there has been an important move away from a limited view of quality control, towards a broader view of 'quality management'. This move has been so dramatic that many people have referred to the 'quality revolution'. There seem to be four main reasons why this has occurred:

- improved processes can guarantee products with consistently high quality;
- organizations use high quality to gain a competitive advantage;
- consumers have become accustomed to high-quality products and are now unwilling to accept anything less;
- organizations can reduce costs by improving quality.

The fundamental job of any organization is to supply products that satisfy customer demand. When given the choice, customers always opt for higher-quality products, so any organization that ignores the trend towards higher quality will lose out to competitors that are better at meeting customer expectations. Although high quality will not guarantee the success of a product, low quality will certainly guarantee its failure. It follows that the main benefit of producing high-quality products is staying in business (see Figure 9.2). Other benefits include:

■ enhanced reputation;
■ competitive advantage;
■ a reduction in the amount of marketing needed;
■ improvement in sales and market share;
■ a rise in productivity;
■ improvement in long-term profitability;
■ a reduction in liability for defective products;
■ a reduction in waste;
■ a reduction in costs.

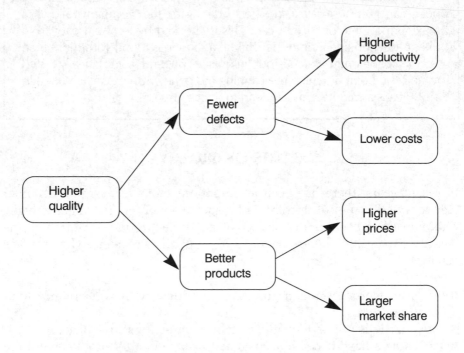

Figure 9.2 *Some benefits from higher quality*

Most of these are fairly obvious, but the idea that increasing quality can reduce costs is particularly interesting. This goes against the traditional view that increased quality can only be bought at a higher cost. It seems obvious that making a higher-quality product uses more time, more careful operations, a more skilful workforce, better materials, and so on. However, some of the wider costs are actually reduced when quality is increased.

If a washing machine is sold with a faulty part, the customer will complain and the manufacturer will arrange for the machine to be repaired under its warranty. The manufacturer could have saved money by finding the fault before the machine left the factory, and it could have saved even more by designing a machine that did not have a fault in the first place. The implication is that organizations can save money by making products of a higher quality.

This can be demonstrated by looking at the costs involved. There are basically four costs of quality – prevention costs, appraisal costs, internal failure costs and external failure costs.

Prevention costs

These are the costs incurred through preventing the occurrence of defects. The quality of a product is set at the design stage, so the best way to guarantee high quality is not by carrying out inspections during the production process, but by designing a good product in the first place. Prevention costs include all aspects of quality that are designed into a product. They include direct costs for the product itself, such as the choice of materials, inclusion of certain features, and the time needed to make the product. They also include indirect costs that depend upon the ease of production, type of process, amount of automation, procurement needed, workforce skill level required, and amount of training needed. The prevention costs are generally incurred through designing a product and process that has high quality.

Appraisal costs

These are the costs of making sure the designed quality is actually achieved. As products move through their process, they are periodically inspected to make sure they reach the quality specified in the design. Related costs include sampling, inspecting, testing and all the other elements of quality control. Generally, the greater amount of effort put into quality control, the higher the end quality of the product, and the higher the costs of achieving this.

Internal failure costs

During the process, some units may be found to have faults, and these are scrapped, returned to an earlier point in the process, repaired, or allowed to continue in the hope that the defect is not important enough to affect the value of the end product. With the exception of the last action (which is not recommended), the alternatives all involve extra work if the unit is to be brought up to a satisfactory quality. Some of the previous work on the unit may also be wasted, as it has to be done again on the repaired unit. The cost of all this work is the internal failure cost – the total cost of making products with defects that are detected somewhere within the process.

The further a product goes through the process, the more money is spent on it and the more expensive it is to scrap or re-work. Ideally, then, defects should be uncovered as early as possible in the process.

A percentage of the internal failure costs comes directly from the loss of material, wasted labour effort, and wasted resources in the defective item. The rest comes from the indirect costs of higher stock levels, longer lead times, the extra capacity needed to allow for defects, and the maintenance of a system to deal with faults.

External failure costs

Producers normally give some kind of guarantee with their products, and are responsible for correcting any faults. If a product goes through the entire production process and is delivered to a customer, who then finds a fault, the faulty unit must be brought back and replaced, re-worked or repaired as necessary. The cost of this work is part of the external failure cost, which is the total cost of making products with defects that are not detected within the process, but are identified by customers.

External failure faults often represent the highest costs of quality management, and should certainly be avoided. In 1982, General Motors had to recall 2.1 million vehicles to repair a small fault, at a cost of over $100 million; in 1994, Ford of America recalled 900,000 vehicles because of a fault in the hand-brake. The cost of such failures can be even higher if producers become liable for damages caused by their defective products; extreme examples of external failure costs include those incurred by the Chernobyl, Three Mile Island and Challenger Space Shuttle disasters.

Minimizing the total cost of quality

The total cost of quality can be calculated by adding together the four separate components. This is quite difficult, mainly because accounting systems do not separate the components and they tend to become lost in other costs. There used to be a widespread view that quality costs were around 5–10 per cent of sales, but more recent estimates have raised this to as much as 20–30 per cent. These can only be estimates, because the overall effects of external failure are very difficult to quantify. If a customer buys a poor product, there are the obvious costs of repair and replacement, but there are also the more elusive costs of lost reputation and lost future sales. Producers today are also being held more responsible for the consequences of defects in their products – surgeons are liable if their negligence during an operation injures a patient; pharmaceutical manufacturers are responsible for any side-effects of their drugs; and management consultants are held responsible for bad advice.

Very high external failure costs – even if they are difficult to calculate exactly – are the reason why the best quality for a product is generally 'perfect quality'. The minimum costs occur when every unit is guaranteed to be free of any faults (shown in Figure 9.3). This is the basis of total quality management (TQM).

TOTAL QUALITY MANAGEMENT (TQM)

It is easy to say that organizations should produce goods of perfect quality, but it is much more difficult to achieve this in practice. One obvious

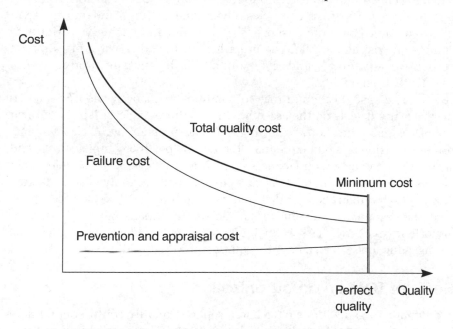

Figure 9.3 *Minimum costs come with perfect quality*

approach is to use more rigorous inspections for quality control, but this is not a perfect solution as it can miss some defects. In recent years there has been a more radical approach, represented by the view that 'you can't inspect quality into a product'.

The central idea of total quality management (TQM) is that managing quality is an integral part of all operations. If a customer goes to a tailor and orders a suit, he will only be satisfied if the suit is well designed and well made, if there are no faults in the material used, if the price is reasonable, if the salesperson is helpful, and if the shop is pleasant. This means that everyone at the tailor's business – from the person who designs the suit to the person who sells it, and from the person who owns the organization to the person who keeps it clean – is directly involved in the quality of the end product.

> With Total Quality Management, the whole organization works together to guarantee, and systematically improve, product quality.
> The aim is to make products of perfect quality – with zero defects.

A significant amount of work on TQM has been done by Japanese manufacturers since the 1940s. Japanese industry had been disrupted by wars, their plant and equipment were out of date, productivity was low, and their domestic markets had been destroyed. Japan started to rebuild its industry by making cheap imitations of products from other countries, and exporting them to more prosperous countries. Over time, living standards in Japan rose, operating costs increased and it became increasingly difficult to compete on cost alone. Manufacturers looked for other ways of gaining a competitive advantage, and they found this by making products with consistently high quality.

By the 1980s, studies found that air conditioners made in the USA had 70 times as many defects on the assembly line as those made in Japan, and had 17 times as many breakdowns in the first year of operation. A US manufacturer of television sets had more than 150 defects per 100 completed sets, and was trying to compete with Japanese companies that averaged 0.5 defects per 100 sets. US manufacturers of car components had warranty costs that were ten times higher than those of their Japanese counterparts. Not surprisingly – and despite economic problems in the late 1990s – Japanese industry came to dominate many world markets, including motorcycles, consumer electronics, cars, machine tools, steel, computer equipment, ship-building and banks.

Effects of TQM on an organization

Traditionally, organizations have had a separate quality control department to inspect the work of production departments. These two functions had completely different objectives: production would try to make products as quickly as possible, while quality control inspected products to make sure they met specifications, possibly by slowing down production. This inevitably led to damaging conflicts, with one department seen as benefiting only at the expense of the other.

More recently, organizations have changed their approach to quality management, and moved the emphasis from inspections at the end of production, to focus on the following:

- operations during the process itself, to make sure no defects are made; and
- the planning stages, to make sure the design of the product and the process allow high quality.

Now, quality management is no longer a separate function concentrating on the later parts of a process, but an integral part of the process, concentrating on the earlier parts. In effect, operational departments have taken responsibility for their own quality.

This has had a significant effect on people working on the process. Each person is now responsible for passing on only products that are of perfect quality. If someone finds a fault, it means that something has gone wrong; they have the authority to stop the process and investigate. They are empowered to find the reason for the fault, and to suggest ways of avoiding it in the future. This is called 'quality at source', with 'job enlargement' for each person; now, everyone is responsible both for his or her previous job and for an inherent quality management function.

It is interesting to compare this approach of quality at source with the traditional view, which only allowed the process to stop as a last resort. Then, nobody working on the line could stop it; if they had a problem, they could report to a manager, who would make a decision, or pass the details to higher managers for a decision. Often there was a suggestion that any problems must be caused by people not working properly, so it is not surprising that faults were often ignored or hidden. The cause of the problem would then go unnoticed until it became much more serious.

One of the themes of TQM is that decision-making is devolved to those most closely involved. People working directly on the process often have a clearer idea of what is needed than those working some distance away. Moving this responsibility down to the workforce means that fewer supervisors are needed, and the organization becomes 'flatter'. Fewer quality inspectors are also needed, and they can now focus on their training and facilitating roles.

The changes in responsibility are reflected in the way that people are rewarded. Many people were traditionally paid for making high volumes, often regardless of quality, but TQM says that they should also be paid for quality. This encourages them to take an interest in how well they make the product, and to look actively for improvements. These suggestions for changes might be collected in suggestion boxes, at informal progress meetings, or in 'quality circles', in which groups of people meet regularly to discuss ways of improving the operations.

Of course, devolving responsibility to lower levels of the workforce can lead to problems. It only really works properly with the following assets:

- a well-educated workforce that is capable of recognizing, analysing and solving problems;
- people who are able and willing to exchange ideas;
- people who see themselves as working for the good of the organization;
- a management that is willing to share information on costs and operations.

Some of the main differences introduced by TQM are summarized in Table 9.1.

Implementing total quality management

If TQM is to be implemented, fundamental changes must be made in the way that an organization works. The introduction of TQM is a major step that needs careful planning. Perhaps the first step is to appoint a team that can manage the changes. This team might start by examining the present position of the organization, and finding out what changes are needed before TQM may be introduced, and how these changes might be achieved.

Table 9.1 *Changing views of quality management*

Criteria	Traditional attitude	Attitude with TQM
Importance	quality is a technical issue	quality is a strategic issue
Cost	high quality costs money	high quality saves money
Responsibility	quality control department	everyone in the organization
Target	meet specifications	continuous improvement
Measured by	average quality level	zero defects
Emphasis	detecting defects	preventing defects
Attitude	inspect quality in	build quality in
Defined by	organization	customers

In other words, the team designs a plan for implementing TQM, which describes the present situation, the direction in which the organization must move, specific goals to measure progress in this direction, a timetable of activities needed to change the organization, and the resources needed to achieve these changes. The team does not, of course, implement TQM itself, but it helps the rest of the organization to make the necessary changes; the team is a planner and facilitator rather than a 'doer'.

In practical terms, an organization needs to take seven steps in order to implement TQM.

1. Get top-management commitment. Managers control the organization, and they must be convinced that TQM is not another management fad, but a new way of thinking that will really improve performance.
2. Find out what customers want. This goes beyond simply asking for their opinions, and gets them involved in the process, perhaps discussing designs in focus groups.
3. Design products with quality in mind. The aim is to come up with products that meet or exceed customer expectations.
4. Design the process with quality in mind. Quality must be considered at all points in the process so that high-quality products can be guaranteed.
5. Build teams of empowered employees. Recognize that employees really are an organization's most valuable asset and make sure they are trained, motivated and able to produce high-quality products.
6. Keep track of results. Set quality targets and measure progress towards these; use benchmarks to compare performance with other organizations, and strive for continuous improvement.
7. Extend these ideas to suppliers and distributors.

These steps may seem straightforward, but they require considerable effort. Implementing TQM can take many years of effort and continuous improvement, so it is not surprising that organizations fail along the way. There are many reasons for these failures, including:

- lack of management commitment;
- lack of planning;
- managers not really changing their habits;
- the workforce not really becoming involved;
- the implementation becoming bogged down or too bureaucratic;
- changes being unpopular; and
- managers being satisfied with small improvements.

Edwards Deming, one of the 'quality gurus', was concerned that many organizations did not get the benefits they expected from TQM. To help them on their way, he compiled a list of 14 principles that represented important guidelines.

Deming's 14 points

1. Create constancy of purpose towards product quality.
2. Refuse to accept customary levels of mistakes, delays, defects and errors.
3. Stop depending on mass inspection, but build quality into the product in the first place.
4. Stop awarding business on the basis of price only – reduce the number of suppliers and insist on meaningful measures of quality.
5. Develop programmes for continuous improvement of costs, quality, productivity and service.
6. Institute training for all employees.
7. Focus supervision on helping employees to do a better job.
8. Drive out fear by encouraging two-way communication.
9. Break down barriers between departments and encourage problem-solving through teamwork.
10. Eliminate numerical goals, posters and slogans that demand improvements without saying how these should be achieved.
11. Eliminate arbitrary quotas that interfere with quality.
12. Remove barriers that stop people having pride in their work.
13. Institute vigorous programmes of life-long education, training and self-improvement.
14. Put everyone to work on implementing these 14 points.

Deming's 14 points is not a programme that has a fixed duration, but the points do lead to a new way of thinking in organizations. They emphasize the fact that managers are in control of the organization and are responsible for improving its performance; and, conversely, that if the organization is performing badly, managers are still responsible and should take the blame. This view considers a process with two parts:

■ the system, over which managers have control, and which contributes 85 per cent of the variation in quality;
■ the workers, who are under their own control, and who contribute 15 per cent of the variation in quality.

Major improvements in quality come from managers improving the system rather than workers improving their own performance. This is similar to productivity, in which the best improvements do not come from making people work harder, but from improving the design of the process.

Another important point in Deming's list is that every individual should be properly trained for his or her job. When Ford of America introduced TQM, it sent over 6,000 people to training courses in two years. The company recognized that it could only make good products if it had good components, so it also trained 1,000 suppliers and gave a clear statement that it would only consider suppliers whose approach to quality matched its own.

This view relating to suppliers has become a common one, and the ISO 9000 family of standards is a formal qualification that shows that suppliers can give consistent quality. ISO certification is administered by independent third parties who check the quality management procedures used by the organization, and then make sure that these procedures are actually being used. Some people think that the standards guarantee high product quality, but in reality they show only that an organization has introduced a programme of quality management, and that the product quality is consistent and reliable. A manufacturer of metal bearings, for example, might specify the tolerance on the diameter of a bearing; ISO certification means that production is within this tolerance, but it does not judge whether the tolerance is good enough for any intended use.

Management example – Oregan Aero

Oregan Aero Ltd is an engine repair company. When Johann Svenson became its president in 1994, the company was very inefficient and heavily dependent on government contracts. By 1996, Svenson realized that Oregan Aero had to change the way it worked if it was going to survive. In particular, he recognized the importance of quality in the industry, and knew that Oregan Aero did not give a high-quality service.

Svenson decided to introduce TQM. For this, he chose a team of nine members from various departments. The team decided that TQM should be gradually phased into the organization, and started with the Turgev TU501 turboprop engine line. The team's first job was to find out what customers really wanted. They spent 3 months and £100,000 doing this. To their surprise, customers' major concerns were not cost and quality, but lead times and ease of doing business. Oregan Aero decided that it wanted to be twice as good as the company that was perceived to be the best in the industry, so it set a target of overhauling a TU501 in 20 days compared with the industry average of 70 days and the industry best of 35 days.

The team simplified and improved the engine overhauling process. They studied the process, critically analysed it and improved it by cutting 91 per cent of non-chargeable steps and 75 per cent of the distance travelled. They divided the line into eight cells with 20 workers each. These workers spent many hours learning about team-building, with training in everything from statistics to running a lathe. As a result, the process was reduced from 221 steps to 57.

When Oregan Aero bid for a £15 million contract to overhaul some gearboxes for the government, its price was 40 per cent lower than the competition, with a much shorter delivery date. At first, the government could not believe the bid, so they sent a team to inspect the company. They were impressed by the improvements, and awarded Oregan the contract. Svenson firmly believes that Oregan only won that contract because of TQM.

CHAPTER REVIEW

- It is difficult to give a general definition of 'quality'. A simple view says that it is the ability to meet, and preferably exceed, customer expectations. A wider view says that overall product quality must be judged by a number of different factors.
- Competition and high customer expectations mean that organizations can only survive if they supply the kind of products that customers want. Customers now demand products with consistently high quality.
- Quality control is the traditional way of achieving high quality. This uses samples, inspections and tests to make sure that planned quality is actually being achieved.
- Quality management is a broader function, which is concerned with all aspects of product quality within an organization.
- There are four costs of quality – prevention, appraisal, internal failure and external failure costs. The last two costs can be very high, but decline with increasing quality. This means that the lowest cost of production comes with products of perfect quality.
- Total quality management focuses the effort of the entire organization on quality. It encourages features such as quality at source, job enlargement and quality circles.
- TQM introduces a new way of thinking to organizations. It requires fundamental changes, but can bring considerable benefits.

FURTHER READING

Crosby, P B (1979) *Quality is Free*, McGraw-Hill, New York, 1979

Kehoe, D F (1996) *The Fundamentals of Quality Management*, Chapman and Hall, London

Peters, T J and Waterman R H (1982) *In Search of Excellence*, Warner Books, New York

Townsend, P L (1992) *Quality in Action*, John Wiley, New York

CHAPTER 10

Measuring and Improving Performance

MEASURES OF PERFORMANCE

In Chapter 9, it was seen that one of the benefits of total quality management (TQM) is an increase in productivity. What exactly is meant by productivity, and is improving it always a good idea? It was also made clear that TQM looks for continuous improvements to operations. This means that organizations must monitor their performance and always look for improvements, but how can they measure performance? And how can they find improvements? This chapter will look for answers to some of these questions.

Every organization needs to measure its performance. This can be done in many ways, including gross profit, profitability, return on investment, market share, number of customers served, share price and productivity. Many of these measures relate to financial performance – perhaps because this is easiest to measure, and because managers are judged on their financial record. From an operations management point of view, a basic measure of performance is capacity. In Chapter 6, it was explained how the designed capacity of a process sets the maximum possible output under ideal conditions, while the effective capacity sets the maximum output under normal working conditions. Two other measures are directly related to capacity: utilization measures the proportion of designed capacity that is actually used; efficiency measures how well the effective capacity is used.

Suppose a particular process has a designed capacity of 100 units a week, but maintenance, set-ups and difficult schedules mean that the effective capacity is only 80 units a week. If the process actually makes 60 units in a week, the results will be as follows:

- utilization = actual output/designed capacity = 60/100 = 0.6 or 60 per cent;
- efficiency = actual output/effective capacity = 60/80 = 0.75 or 75 per cent.

There are many other measures for the performance of operations, including effectiveness, which shows how well the organization is achieving its goals. However, perhaps the most widely used measure is productivity, which measures the amount of output achieved for each unit of resource used. This measure is so important that many organizations have a strategic goal of 'improving productivity'. (Note that all these measures should be treated with caution, as they can give very misleading views.)

Management example – the Johnson-Mead Company

In June 1998, the Johnson-Mead Company had ten people organizing 1,000 specialized life insurance policies for high-risk travellers. In theory, it could process 1,250 policies a month, but breaks, interruptions, holidays, schedules and other factors limited this to about 1,150. The direct costs of this operation were £115,000.

There was growing demand for the service, and in July the company did a small reorganization. After this, it employed 11 people, who could deal with a maximum of 1,600 policies a month, but with a more realistic limit of 1,300. They were a little disappointed to find that in the following month they had only processed 1,200 policies, with direct costs of £156,000. Some measures of this performance are given in Table 10.1.

Table 10.1 *Some measures of performance at the Johnson-Mead Company*

Before reorganization	After reorganization
Number of policies processed per person	
1,000/10 = 100	1,200/11 = 109
Direct costs per policy	
115,000/1,000 = £115	156,000/1,200 = £130
Designed capacity	
1,250	1,600
Effective capacity	
1,150	1,300
Utilization	
1,000/1,250 = 80 per cent	1,200/1,600 = 75 per cent
Efficiency	
1,000/1,150 = 87 per cent	1,200/1,300 = 92 per cent

Even these simple measures have to be interpreted with some care. Johnson-Mead's reorganization increased the number of policies processed per person, but it also increased the direct costs per policy. The capacity has risen along with efficiency, but the utilization has declined. Whether or not this suggests an improved performance depends on the objectives of the company.

The last example shows how different measures of performance can give conflicting views. This is not surprising, as different factors are being measured; it is quite usual for some measures of performance to rise while others decline. When you drive a car faster than usual, the time taken for a journey goes down, but the fuel consumption goes up; if an organization reduces the selling price of a product, the demand increases, but the profit goes down; if it reduces bonus payments, the wage bill will go down, but so will productivity.

An organization should choose its measures of performance carefully, so that they give an accurate view and show how well its goals are being achieved. It must be particularly careful not to use a measure simply because it is easy to find, or because it shows the managers in a good light.

PRODUCTIVITY

Most managers would say that increasing productivity is good – it suggests that costs go down while profits rise. On a national scale, the only way to become more prosperous is by increasing the amount each person produces. In July 1998, Gordon Brown, the Chancellor of the Exchequer, reported that manufacturing productivity in the UK was no higher than it had been in mid-1994, and had actually declined by 1 per cent in the past year. He called for a new 'national economic purpose' to deal with this 'inherited under-performance'. His predecessor, Kenneth Clarke, said in 1993 that there would be 'no pay rise for workers in the public sector unless paid for by increases in productivity'. This may seem reasonable, but it avoids the continuing debate about measures of productivity. How, for example, is it possible to measure – let alone increase – the productivity of a nurse, civil servant or teacher?

Despite such problems, most organizations are continually trying to increase their productivity. They do this primarily because of the competition – there are always competitors who are trying to gain an advantage, and they will attempt to do this by improving their own productivity. It follows that an organization must match a competitor's improvement simply to stay in business. The benefits of higher productivity include:

- long-term survival;
- reduction in costs;
- cutting down on waste of resources;
- increase in profits, wages, real income, and so on;
- targets for improved operations;
- monitoring of improving performance;
- comparisons between operations;
- measurement of management competence.

There are obviously good reasons for organizations to improve productivity, but how can they do this? There are really only four ways:

- improve effectiveness – with better decisions;
- improve efficiency – by designing a better process to give more output with the same inputs;
- improve performance in some other way – such as reducing waste through higher quality, fewer accidents, less disruption;
- improve morale – to give more co-operation and incentives.

The old-fashioned idea of 'getting people to work harder' has very little to do with productivity. A person digging a hole with a spade can work very hard and still be far less productive than a lazy person with a bulldozer. In general, about 85 per cent of productivity is set by the process, which is designed by management, and only about 15 per cent is under the control of individual workers. Productivity is, therefore, largely a measure of management performance and depends far less on individual effort.

Definitions

It would be useful here to clarify exactly what is meant by productivity. It has already been said that it is the amount of output produced for each unit of resource used. To be more precise, total productivity is the total output divided by the total input:

$$\text{Total productivity} = \frac{\text{total output}}{\text{total input}}$$

Unfortunately, this definition has a number of drawbacks. To start with, the input and output must be in the same units, and this usually means that they are translated into a common currency. The amounts depend on the accounting conventions used, and there is no longer an objective measure. Another problem is that, for a reliable measure of total productivity, all inputs and outputs should be included. Finding the values of all the inputs and outputs is not easy. Some inputs, such as water and sunlight, are difficult to evaluate, as are some outputs, such as waste and pollution.

Because of these difficulties, most organizations do not use measures of total productivity, but substitute some other measures of partial productivity. These show the total output divided by one kind of input. Typical examples of partial productivity are the amount produced per person, the output per machine-hour, the amount produced per kilowatt-hour of electricity, or the amount made for each pound of investment.

$$\text{Partial productivity} = \frac{\text{total output}}{\text{one input}}$$

To simplify the calculation even further, the 'total output' only includes production and does not include secondary outputs such as waste and scrap.

The partial productivity measures are usually related to four types of resource:

- equipment productivity, such as units made per machine-hour, sales per checkout, or miles driven per vehicle;
- labour productivity, such as units made per person, tonnes produced per shift, or orders shipped per hour worked;
- capital productivity, such as units made for each pound of investment, sales per unit of capital, or production per pound invested in equipment;
- energy productivity, such as units of output per kilowatt-hour of electricity, units made for each pound spent on energy, or value of output per barrel of oil used.

Whichever measure of productivity is used, it should give a reliable view of the performance of the organization. It would, for example, make little sense to measure the productivity of an automatic telephone exchange by measuring the number of calls per employee, or the productivity of a bank by measuring the number of transactions per kilowatt-hour of electricity consumed. This seems obvious, but many organizations have ignored this simple advice. Over many years, the reported productivity of British Coal, for example, rose quite dramatically. Unfortunately, the standard measure of productivity was tonnes of coal mined per shift. Increasing automation led to apparently higher productivity, but this hid the fact that the industry was in a long-term decline, as it had difficulty competing with imported coal and alternative fuels.

Any single measure of productivity gives only one, limited view of the organization. For a broader view, several measures, relating to different aspects of operations, are needed. Unfortunately, this can be quite difficult. For example, the productivity of universities is often judged by the number of full-time equivalent students per member of staff. However, to give a broader view it would be necessary also to measure the academic standards, teaching quality, research skills, contributions to knowledge, community service, support of local business, and so on. Measuring performance in these areas is largely a matter of judgement, so it is very difficult to give a convincing overall measure for productivity. This is even more difficult with services such as the police, the army and the fire service, which are most 'successful' if they do not work at all – in other words, if there are no crimes, wars or fires.

To give a reasonable view of actual performance, a measure of productivity must:

- relate to the organization's objectives;
- focus on significant factors;
- be measurable;
- be reasonably objective;
- be agreed by everyone concerned;
- use consistent units.

So, it is clear that it may not always be a good idea to increase productivity. If an organization uses an inappropriate measure, increasing productivity might have no effect on real performance, and might actually be damaging. Different measures of productivity can also give contradictory views, so that increasing the use of automation, for example, may increase labour productivity but reduce capital productivity. This means that the definitions used must be considered very carefully before making any decisions based on productivity figures.

COMPARING PERFORMANCE

Sensible measures of productivity, or any other measures, should give a reasonable view of an organization's performance. These measures can be used for:

- comparing the current performance of the organization with its performance in the past;
- making comparisons with other organizations;
- comparing the performance of different parts of the organization;
- making decisions about investments and proposed changes to the process;
- measuring the effects of changes;
- helping with other internal functions, such as wage negotiations;
- highlighting areas where performance should be improved.

Measures of performance are normally used for some kind of comparison, because absolute measures often have no real meaning. For example, the fact that a shop has annual sales of £1,200 per square metre does not indicate whether it is doing well or badly, unless the figure is compared to those of comparable shops. Most measures are used to compare the organization's actual performance with some agreed standard measures. There are four sources for these standards:

- absolute standards, which give the best performance that could ever be achieved. This is a target at which to aim, such as the goal of TQM, which is to have zero defects;
- target performance – a more realistic target that is agreed by managers, who want to set a tough, but attainable level of performance. The absolute standard for the number of customer complaints received each week is zero, but a more realistic, agreed target might be one;
- historical standards, which look at performance that has actually been achieved in the past. Historical standards show the performance that can be achieved if there is no improvement; as organizations are always looking for improvements, this can be viewed as the worst performance that might be accepted;
- competitors' standards, which show the performance actually being achieved by competitors. This is the lowest level of performance that an organization must achieve to remain competitive. Federal Express, for example, delivers packages 'absolutely, positively overnight', so other delivery services must achieve at least this standard if they are to compete.

Benchmarking

When an organization compares its performance with a competitor, the practice is called 'benchmarking'. To be more specific, benchmarking compares an organization's performance with the best operations in the industry. There are several steps in benchmarking, which starts by identifying which competitor has the best of the following:

- cost per unit;
- processing time per unit;
- market share;
- return on investment;
- customer retention;
- revenue per unit;
- customer satisfaction; or
- some other measures of performance.

Then, the competitor's operations are examined, to see how it achieves this superior performance (see Figure 10.1).

Benchmarking allows an organization to set realistic performance targets, and it shows how these targets can be met. To be blunt, organizations use benchmarking in order to find ideas and ways of doing operations that they can copy or adapt.

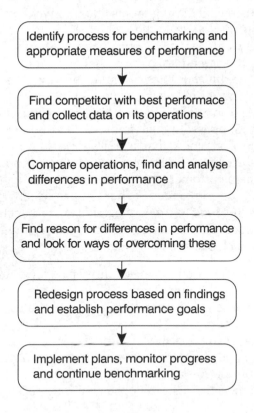

Figure 10.1 *Procedure for benchmarking*

There are several variations on the basic ideas of benchmarking. Usually, an organization will look at its main competitors and see how they organize their operations, but sometimes it will use different internal divisions to see what one can learn from another. It might also look at different types of organization, so that a train operator might learn something from looking at bus operators, airlines, or even companies that give a high level of customer service, such as supermarkets.

Management example – benchmarking in banks

In 1998, the *Sunday Times* printed a number of articles that were critical of the high-street banks. Cases were reported in which banks had overcharged customers, made mistakes, been negligent, or had simply not given their customers a reasonable level of service. These articles brought a huge response from readers who had complaints about their banks, and the *Sunday Times* concluded that the big banks were so absorbed with making profits that they were 'probably the least popular private institutions in the country'.

Some banks were clearly working against customers' interests. One, for example, threatened to punish staff who told customers about accounts that paid higher rates of interest than their existing deposits. Several banks offered high-interest deposit accounts for a short time, and then locked in the money for long periods, giving much lower interest rates. Supposedly, high-interest, 30-, 60- or 90-day notice accounts were a gimmick that actually paid lower rates than other instant-access accounts. Banks also stopped co-operating with agents who tried to help customers get the lowest possible bank charges.

The overall performance of banks was clearly not satisfying customers, so the *Sunday Times* suggested some benchmarks – based on industry practices – in order to set some minimum standards for service. These included the following:

- telling customers of any changes in their interest rates at the time when the changes are made;
- giving comparisons between existing account rates and alternative, suitable accounts;
- publishing all charges clearly, including fees;
- telling customers if instant-access accounts pay higher interest rates than 30- , 60- or 90-day notice accounts; and
- giving customers the right to negotiate through agents.

PROCESS IMPROVEMENT

Process charts

Organizations should look for continuous improvements to their process, but how can they set about effecting these improvements? An obvious first step – often ignored – is to describe the details of the existing process. This has the following advantages:

- making sure that everyone involved understands the process and its purpose;
- giving a starting point from which new designs can be developed;
- highlighting problems with the existing process that should be overcome;
- giving standards for judging new plans.

A convenient way of describing a process is to use some kind of process chart. There are several possible formats for such a chart, but each breaks down the process into a sequence of separate activities and shows the relationships between those activities. For example, when a patient visits a doctor's surgery, the process might involve the following activities:

- entering and talking to the receptionist;
- sitting down and waiting until called;
- when called, going to the doctor's room;
- discussing problems with the doctor;
- when finished, leaving the doctor's room;
- talking to the receptionist and leaving.

This can be drawn as the informal precedence diagram shown in Figure 10.2.

This informal chart gives a general view of the process, but it does not give many details. A better approach looks at the types of activities and describes each as follows:

- operation – where something is actually done;
- movement – where products are moved;
- storage – where products are put away until they are needed;
- delay – where products are held up;
- inspection – which tests the quality of the product.

Now it is possible to draw a more useful chart of a process, using six steps. The first three steps describe the current process, while the last three look for improvements. (The first three steps give a detailed description of a

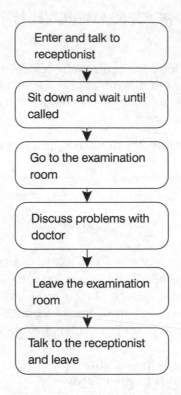

Figure 10.2 *Informal process chart for a visit to the doctor*

process; an example of a chart is shown in Figure 10.3. Steps 1 and 2 can probably be done by observation, while step 3 is a calculation. The next part of the analysis looks for improvements to the process.)

1. Look at the process and list all the activities in their proper sequence, from the start of the process through to the finish.
2. Classify each activity as an operation, movement, inspection, delay or storage. Find the time taken and distance moved in each step.
3. Summarize the process by adding the number of each type of activity, the total time for the process, the rate of carrying out each operation, and any other relevant information.
4. Critically analyse each operation, asking questions such as, 'Can we eliminate this activity?', 'How can we improve this operation?', 'Can we reduce the distance moved or the time spent?', 'Can we combine activities?'

5. Based on this analysis, revise the process. This should aim at simplifying the process, by having fewer operations, eliminating delays, reducing times for operations, moving shorter distances, eliminating duplicated jobs, using TQM and designing products that are easy to make. But make sure that each operation can still give the output needed by the process. If there are bottlenecks or inefficient activities, look for improvements to remove these.

6. Check the new process and test it, prepare everyone for changes, train staff, and then implement the changes.

Figure 10.3 shows a process chart that has been drawn using the first three steps. This can be used to look for some improvements to the process. First, it is possible to see that the output is set by the activity that takes the most time. Step number 16 – finishing the product – is the longest, at 5.5 minutes, so the maximum output from the process is 60/5.5, or 10.9 units

Process chart	- Part 421/302	Operation	Movement	Inspection	Delay	Storage	Time (mins)	Distance (metres)	Comments
Step number	Description								
1	Fetch component		X				2.5	50	
2	Put components on machine	X					2		
3	Start machine	X					1.2		
4	Fetch sub-assembly		X				3	40	
5	Wait for machine to stop				X		5.2		
6	Unload machine	X					2		
7	Inspect result			X			1.5		
8	Join sub-assembly	X					5		
9	Move unit to machine		X				2.5	25	
10	Load machine to start	X					2		
11	Wait for machine to stop				X		5		
12	Unload machine	X					1.4		
13	Carry unit to inspection area		X				2	25	
14	Inspect and test			X			5.2		
15	Carry unit to finish area		X				1.4	20	
16	Finish unit	X					5.5		
17	Final inspection			X			3.5		
18	Carry unit to store		X				5.3	45	
Summary:		#							
	Operations	7					19.1		
	Movements	6					16.7	205	
	Inspections	3					10.2		
	Delays	2					10.2		
	Storage	0					0		
Totals:		18					56.2	205	

Figure 10.3 *Example of a process chart*

an hour. If the planned output is higher than this, the process must be changed, perhaps adding more finishers or changing the way the finishing is done.

Steps 5 and 11 have a delay of 10.2 minutes. This wasted time should be reduced, perhaps by better planning or by using equipment in a different way. In steps 1, 4, 9, 13, 15 and 18, the product moves a total of 205 metres, taking 16.7 minutes. This should be reduced, perhaps by improving the layout.

The most effective way of improving a process is to remove the activities that contribute nothing. As Peter Drucker has said, 'There is no greater waste than doing absolutely perfectly that which doesn't have to be done at all.'

Management example – conference registration

Some processes are so bad that it will only take a little thought to achieve improvements. Unfortunately, there is often nobody in the organization who has the time or incentive to make the changes, so things continue in the usual inefficient way.

The autumn 1998 conference of the International Management Association had 2,100 delegates. All of these people had to register, using a procedure that had been used for several years. This started with delegates queueing to pick up registration documents at an information booth, and then walking 30m to the hotel reception, where they formed another queue at the front desk. Here, a receptionist checked the delegates' details, confirmed their hotel booking and gave them information about the hotel and their room.

Then the delegates went up two floors, walked 120m to the conference administrators, and joined a queue to have their registration forms checked, see what sessions and functions they planned to attend, and what special arrangements they needed. Then they walked 50m to the conference registrar's office, where a clerk calculated any fees they had to pay and handed over tickets and information about the various functions. Then, the delegates walked 30m to a cashier's window to pay their fees and get a receipt.

If delegates wanted car parking at the hotel, they had to go to the parking desk, which was 150m from the cashier. Anyone who wanted any other special arrangements had to visit other areas.

Completing the registration took well over an hour, and delegates had to walk an average of 400m. One annoyed delegate suggested a streamlined process in which they would walk 30m and take an average of ten minutes.

Other types of chart

Process charts are useful in describing and analysing a process, but they do not show what each participant in the process is doing at any time, or how they interact. A convenient format for showing this is a multiple activity chart. This is a form of Gantt chart, which has a timescale down the side of the diagram, and all the participants listed across the top. The time each participant works on the process is blocked off. Figure 10.4 shows an example of a multiple activity chart for two typists working on word processors and connected to a single high-quality printer. This shows both the total time that participants are busy during a process, and how this time is distributed. If the operators are idle for long periods they can be assigned to other jobs, but this is not possible if they are idle for a number of short periods.

People sometimes find it difficult to see how a process can be improved, especially if they have been working very closely with it. Two other diagrams identify areas for improvement by identifying where problems occur.

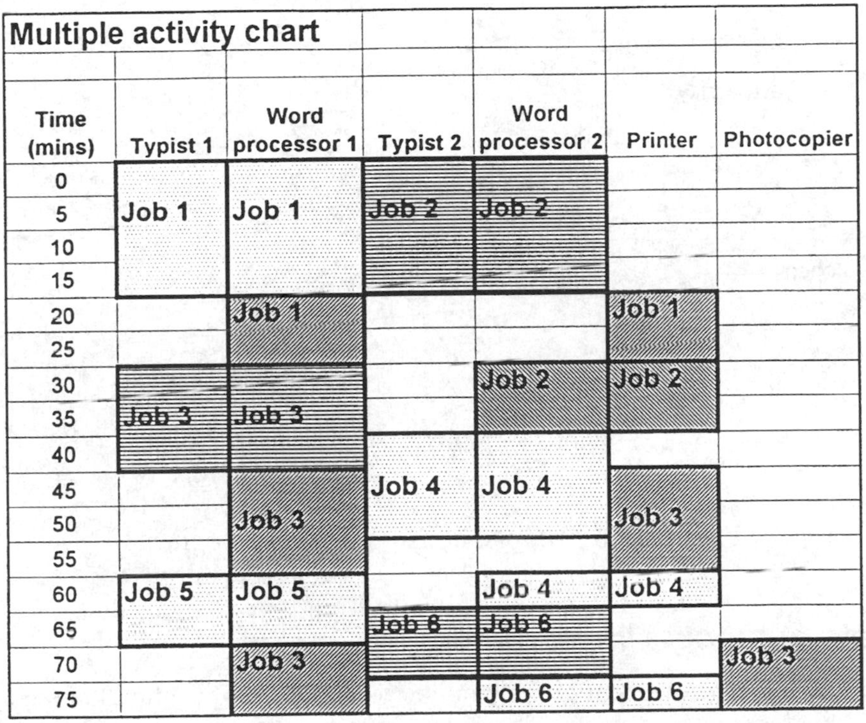

Multiple activity chart					
Time (mins)	Typist 1	Word processor 1	Typist 2	Word processor 2	Printer	Photocopier
0	Job 1	Job 1	Job 2	Job 2		
5	Job 1	Job 1	Job 2	Job 2		
10						
15						
20		Job 1			Job 1	
25						
30				Job 2	Job 2	
35	Job 3	Job 3				
40						
45		Job 3	Job 4	Job 4		
50					Job 3	
55						
60	Job 5	Job 5		Job 4	Job 4	
65			Job 6	Job 6		
70		Job 3				Job 3
75			Job 6	Job 6		

Figure 10.4 *Multiple activity chart for typists*

A cause-and-effect diagram shows the possible causes of a problem in a simple 'fish-bone' diagram. If a customer complains in a hamburger restaurant, it is a sign that something has gone wrong and the process needs adjusting. The problem might be caused by raw materials, cooking, staff or facilities. Problems with the staff might, in turn, be caused by their skills, availability, or attitude to work. Then, problems with the availability of staff might be caused by the number of people available or the times that they work, and so on. Figure 10.5 shows part of a cause-and-effect diagram demonstrating these relationships.

Pareto charts are based on the observation that 80 per cent of problems come from 20 per cent of causes. For example, Woolworth will find that 80 per cent of customer complaints come from 20 per cent of their products. A Pareto chart is simply a bar chart of the frequency of different problems, and this highlights the areas of the process that need special attention.

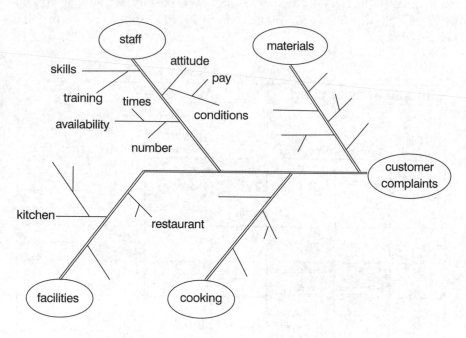

Figure 10.5 *Part of a cause-and-effect diagram*

Rate of process improvement

Continuous improvement of the kind suggested by TQM is often known by its Japanese name 'kaizen'. This suggests a continuous stream of small improvements, with the accumulated effects over time leading to dramatic improvements in performance. The emphasis is on relatively small incremental changes, which can be absorbed by the process, give few disruptions, and cause no major problems with things going seriously wrong. The continuing changes also build a momentum for improvement, which makes sure that the process is always getting better.

This incremental approach does have its critics, who say that continually tinkering with a process gives an impression of uncertainty and lack of

---

Management example – Freemantle Restaurant

The Freemantle Restaurant is a well-established business near the centre of Manchester. It has a healthy demand for its high-quality, expensive business lunches and dinners. Paul Samson is the owner of Freemantle, and looks after all the administration personally. Although there are few complaints from customers, Samson always keeps a record of them. Over the past three years, he has collected the figures shown in Figure 10.6.

Cause	Number of complaints	Percentage of complaints
Faults in the bill	80	51
Slow service	31	20
Smokers too near non-smokers	19	12
Comfort of the chairs	11	7
Wine	5	3
Temperature of the restaurant	5	3
Wait for a table	2	1
Too limited menu	2	1
Food – ingredients used	2	1
Food – cooking	1	1

Figure 10.6 shows a Pareto chart, which summarizes Paul Samson's results and clearly identifies the main problem areas at the Freemantle Restaurant. There are almost no complaints about the food, so customers are clearly pleased with what they are eating. Over half of the complaints come from faults in the bill, so procedures here should be improved. Sometimes, the service is slow, especially at busy times. By dealing with these two areas, Samson could remove the cause of almost three-quarters of customer complaints. Providing more comfortable chairs and increasing the size of the non-smoking area would deal with another 19 per cent of complaints.

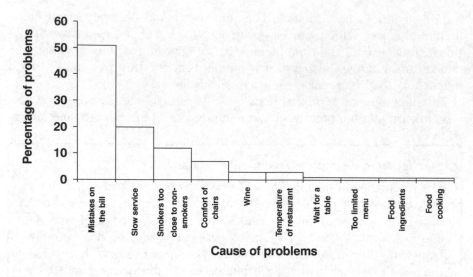

Figure 10.6 *Pareto chart for the Freemantle Restaurant*

leadership. It might also move the process in the wrong direction, as an attractive small change might block the way for much bigger gains in another, more beneficial direction. The major criticism, however, is that incremental changes do not get to the root of problems and fail to look for dramatic improvements. Making small adjustments to a process that is fundamentally bad will still leave a bad process. The critics say that organizations should not look so hard for improvements to the current process, but should put more effort into looking for an ideal process and into designing operations that come as close to this ideal as possible. This would lead to a fundamental, sudden and dramatic change in operations – typical of the breakthrough that comes when introducing new technology. Perhaps the best-known approach of this kind is business process re-engineering (BPR).

> Business process re-engineering is the fundamental rethinking and radical redesign of business processes to achieve dramatic improvements in critical, contemporary measures of performance, such as cost, quality, service and speed.
>
> (Michael Hammer)

Business process re-engineering focuses the organization on the whole process of supplying products for customers. It is a useful way of summarizing several related ideas. Some of its main principles are:

- a process should be designed across functions and allow work to flow naturally through the process – in other words, organizations should concentrate on the whole process rather than on the separate activities that make up the process;
- managers should strive for dramatic improvements in performance by radically rethinking and redesigning the process – the key is 'discontinuous thinking';
- information technology is fundamental to re-engineering, as it allows radical new solutions to problems;
- work should be done where it makes most sense – so information processing becomes a part of the process rather than a separate function, and the internal customers for a product should become responsible for making the product themselves;
- decisions are made where the work is done, and by those doing the work – so that work, supervision and control become different aspects of the process, which can be merged;
- it is not necessary to be an 'expert' to help redesign a process, and being an outsider without preconceived ideas often helps.

BPR is an approach to change rather than a formal procedure, so it is not possible to say that 'this is how to re-engineer a process'. Perhaps because of this, organizations have mixed experiences with its implementation. Some have reported outstanding results – for example, the early work in the IBM Credit Corporation increased output by a factor of 100 – but around three-quarters of organizations trying BPR have not had the success they were hoping for. James Champy, who described some basic work with Michael Hammer, soon agreed that 're-engineering is in trouble'. There are many reasons why organizations have not enjoyed success when trying to use re-engineering. They might, for example:

- try to adjust a process rather than fundamentally redesigning it;
- settle for minor improvements;
- stop before all the work is done;
- pull back when they meet resistance to change;
- fail to put sufficient resources into the BPR;
- fail to give senior management support;
- appoint a leader who is not interested;
- set up a separate and remote working group;
- bury BPR in other initiatives.

So, one of the main criticisms of BPR is that it promises a lot, but in practice might deliver very little. Other criticisms include the following:

- realistically, it is very difficult to achieve the dramatic improvements promised by BPR;
- sudden changes to the process can be very disruptive and expensive;
- dramatic changes might use new technology of which the organization has no experience;
- a new process can take a long time to settle down before it starts working properly;
- BPR is seen as the latest management fad and is not taken seriously;
- it always uses a radical approach, even when minor adjustments would be best;
- it emphasizes staff reductions, and can become an excuse for getting rid of workers;
- it can put short-term goals of cost reduction ahead of longer-term interests;
- radical redesign and downsizing may lead to the organization losing essential experience;
- re-engineered organizations can be vulnerable to changes in the environment.

Management example – SW Kobi Electricity

SW Kobi Electricity (SWK) supplies electricity to around 400,000 domestic users. Every 3 months, a meter reader is sent around to all its customers. The meter readings are passed to the accounts department, which calculates the bill. This process has remained essentially the same for many years. Originally, the whole process was manual, but now the meter readers carry a hand-held terminal. They enter the current reading into this, and at the end of the day this is plugged into the accounts department's computer, which automatically prints the bills.

Despite continual improvements, the process of reading meters is still labour-intensive. SWK was looking at ways of reducing the number of meter readers, perhaps by improving the hand-held terminals, sending out estimated bills every other period, or combining with other utility companies to have joint meter readers. Then they decided to investigate a more radical, re-engineered approach. Most customers had telephones and bank accounts, and SWK could use these for a completely new system. They could install 'intelligent' meters linked to the telephone lines, and have their computers automatically interrogate the meters every 3 months, or however often customers wanted. Then the computers could link into bank accounts and automatically deduct the amount owing. This would eliminate almost all the meter readers and the accounts department.

Unfortunately, as with many apparently good ideas, progress on this system has encountered a number of snags. Many customers are not happy with the idea of automatic billing, and are even less happy about automatic withdrawal of money from their bank accounts. The banks realize that electricity bills cause many complaints, and they will not accept a new system that will get them involved with these problems.

MOTIVATING EMPLOYEES

The importance of good relations between all employees cannot be over-stated, and the old cliché that, for any process, 'an organization's most important asset is its employees' is still true. One way of increasing productivity and performance is to motivate people to work better and more efficiently. It is obviously a simplification to say that 'a happy worker is a productive worker', but there is none the less a certain amount of truth in this.

One of the major problems with re-engineering – and with other approaches that emphasize reductions in numbers of employees – is that they consider the workforce to be a drain on the organization. This inevitably causes some conflict between managers, who are trying to design a process that needs fewer people, and employees, who are trying to keep their jobs. This tension is not healthy, and the performance of the organization will inevitably decline. This is not a new observation; it has been causing difficulties since the development of assembly lines at the beginning of the twentieth century. Henry Ford essentially re-engineered the process of assembling cars by having people working in a line and repeating the same simple job many times – perhaps thousands of times – a day. These assembly lines brought advantages to the organization, which could then:

- employ unskilled or low-skilled people;
- train those people quickly to do the simple jobs;
- pay low wages;
- achieve high output; and
- control the flow of work.

Unfortunately, this division of labour – in which each person endlessly repeats a small job – has serious problems. The main one is that people find the work boring, tiring and unsatisfying. They have no chance of snowing initiative, gaining promotion, communicating with colleagues, or having control over their work. The result is a workforce that lacks motivation and has a low morale. This in turn leads to low productivity, absenteeism, grievances and high staff turnover. Although they were often successful, these assembly lines could not, in practice, guarantee high productivity.

It is surprisingly difficult to list the factors that make a job attractive, so that people find it rewarding, work harder and are more productive. Some people like work that pays a lot; others like challenges; some people like to 'do good', or to be recognized; some like to socialize, while others like to be left alone. It is vital to look at employees' needs and ask the fundamental question, 'Why do people work?' McGregor suggested two answers for this, which he called Theory X and Theory Y.

- Theory X – assumes that people are essentially lazy, dislike work, lack ambition and avoid responsibility. They will only work because they have to. This means that organizations can only get people to work by using close supervision, threats, punishments, incentives, and so on. This theory does not explain why people work beyond their retirement age, do voluntary work, continue to work after they have won the lottery, or actually work harder than they need.
- Theory Y – assumes that people work because they like to, considering work to be as natural as rest or play. This means that organizations only have to supply the right conditions, and people will work as effectively as they can.

Both of these views are partly right, but neither gives the whole story. Sometimes, people will only work because they have to, and sometimes the people will work because they want to. In other words, the amount someone works depends on his or her motivation.

- 'Motivation' is difficult to define, but generally a person is said to be 'motivated' when working hard in order to achieve an appropriate goal.

From this definition, it is clear that there are three aspects to motivation. The first is the effort that a person puts into a job – a motivated person will work hard. The second is the perseverance of the effort – a motivated person will continue making an effort for as long as needed. The third is effectiveness – a motivated person will work towards an appropriate goal (see Figure 10.7).

Managers should design jobs that motivate their workers, and this includes considering a number of obvious points:

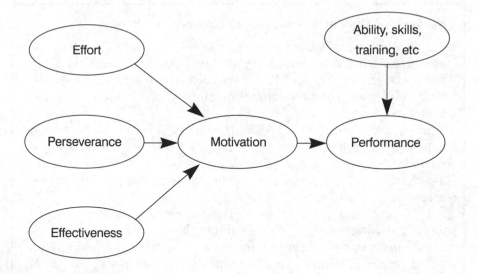

Figure 10.7 *Motivation and performance*

- do not treat people as part of the machinery, but as the most important part of the organization;
- treat people fairly and reward them properly for their work;
- have people working on identifiable and significant parts of the process;
- give broad training for multi-skilled jobs;
- widen work responsibilities to include quality, and so on;
- give meaningful feedback on everyone's performance;
- form employee councils and other ways of participating in management;
- form work teams with authority to make decisions about operations;
- automate dull and dangerous jobs; and
- remove artificial barriers between trades, levels, and so on.

One useful approach that can involve many of these considerations uses self-directed work teams. These are groups of people who have day-to-day responsibility for managing themselves and the process on which they work. Instead of being instructed by supervisors, self-directed work teams take the work to be done, and then schedule their time to achieve this most effectively. This obviously needs a variety of skills within the team, but many organizations have used it both to increase productivity and reduce costs.

Management example – the Magna Employee's Charter

Magna International Inc. is a global supplier of high-technology systems, assemblies and components. In 1998, it had sales of £2.1 billion and a net profit of £125 million. Frank Stronach, the chairman of Magna, believes in fairness and concern for his employees. He has created the Magna Employee's Charter:

Job security – being competitive by making a better product for a better price is the best way to enhance job security. Magna is committed to working together with you to help protect your job. To assist you Magna will provide: job counselling, training and employee assistance programmes.

A safe and healthful workplace – Magna strives to provide you with a working environment which is safe and healthful.

Fair treatment – Magna offers equal employment opportunities based on an individual's qualifications and performance, free from discrimination or favouritism.

Competitive wages and benefits – Magna will provide you with information which will enable you to compare your wages and benefits with those earned by employees of your competitors, as well as with other plants in your community. If your total compensation is found not to be competitive, then your wages will be adjusted.

Employee equity and profit participation – Magna believes that every employee should own a portion of the company.

Communication and information – through regular monthly meetings between management and employees and through publications, Magna will provide you with information so that you will know what is going on in your company and within the industry.

Magna has a hotline to register any complaint if an employee feels that these principles are not being lived up to. It also has an Employee Relations Advisory Board to monitor, advise and make sure that Magna operates within the spirit of the Charter.

CHAPTER REVIEW

■ Every organization needs to measure its performance. There are many possible measures, often emphasizing financial performance. The performance of operations can be measured using capacity, efficiency, utilization, productivity or a number of alternatives.

- Productivity is a widely used measure, which shows the ratio of the output of a process to the inputs. There are many possible definitions of productivity, often emphasizing the use of equipment, labour, capital and energy. Measures of productivity must be carefully designed to give meaningful and reliable results.
- As well as measuring absolute performance, organizations need comparisons of their relative performance. They can base these comparisons on absolute, target, historical, or competitors' performance. Benchmarking is important here, as it compares actual performance with the best achieved in the industry.
- Organizations aim for continuous improvement of their processes. A useful way of looking for these is to give a detailed description of the current process. Several types of process chart can help with this.
- Most organizations look for iterative improvements to their current process. An alternative is to look for dramatic improvements by radically redesigning a process. This is the approach of business process re-engineering, which designs an ideal process from scratch.
- The performance of a process depends directly on the people who work on it. A motivated workforce can be highly productive, and is an organization's most important asset.

FURTHER READING

Drucker, P (1993) *The Practice of Management*, Harper Collins, New York

Gouillant, F and Kelly, J (1995) *Transforming the Organization*, McGraw-Hill, New York

Hammer, M and Champy, J (1993) *Re-engineering the Corporation*, Harper Collins, New York

Kossen, S (1994) *The Human Side of Organizations*, Addison-Wesley, Reading, MA

Leibfried, K H J and McNair, C J (1992) *Benchmarking: a tool for continuous improvement*, Harper Collins, New York

Robbins, H and Finley, M (1997) *Why Change Doesn't Work*, Orion Business Books, London

CHAPTER II

Managing the Supply Chain

LOGISTICS

All operations rely on the efficient movement of people, information and materials. Manufacturers, for example, need a system for bringing in raw materials, consumables, information and services, and then for delivering finished goods to customers; hospitals move patients, materials and other services; the BBC moves actors, cameras, sets, and so on. Organizing the movement of all these resources is the function of logistics.

> Logistics is responsible for the physical movement of all resources through a process.
> It includes procurement of materials from suppliers, movement through the process, delivery to customers, and all associated movements of people, information and services, and all stages in between.

Logistics forms an important link between organizations, as the final product of one becomes the raw material of another. Materials move through a series of organizations, along a supply chain, as shown in Figure 11.1. In practice, this supply chain can be very complicated and even a simple product, such as a cotton shirt, has a long and difficult journey, from the initial supply (raw cotton growing in a field) to its final destination (the shirt on the customer's back). Logistics is responsible for the flow of all materials along this supply chain.

By taking a strategic view of the whole supply chain, an organization can see:

- where it fits in the existing supply chain;
- how it can compete effectively in this position;
- which parts are particularly important for its operations;
- who owns the different parts of the chain;
- which parts of the chain it could usefully expand into;
- the capacities of each part.

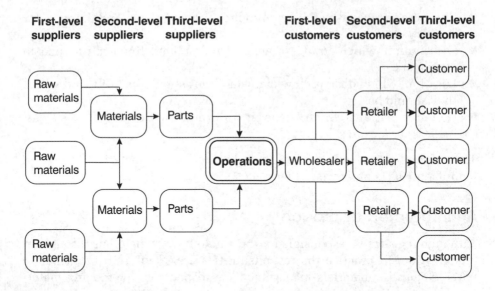

Figure 11.1 *Part of a supply chain*

Functions of logistics

The definition of logistics may be used to take a very broad view – that almost all operations depend on the movement of resources, so logistics is concerned with everything from production planning, through information technology, and on to marketing. Realistically, it is necessary to take a more limited view. It is possible, however, to describe some common functions, even though there are huge differences in the logistics of different organizations – logistics in BP is completely different from logistics in Western National buses, or Barclays Bank, for example. In general, logistics is concerned with the following:

- Procurement or purchasing, which is responsible for buying raw materials from suppliers.
- Traffic and transport, which moves the raw materials from suppliers to the organization's receiving area.
- Receiving, which compares deliveries with orders, unloads delivery vehicles, inspects goods, updates inventory records, etc.
- Warehousing or stores, which stores and monitors materials until needed.
- Inventory control, which deals with the replenishment of stocks and controls inventory levels.
- Material handling, which moves the materials needed for operations during the process.

- Shipping, which takes finished products, checks them, and prepares for delivery.
- Distribution, which arranges transport and delivers finished products to customers.
- Location, which decides how many facilities should be built, and where they should be.
- Communication, which manages information flows and keeps all records for logistics.

These functions are related, as shown by the flow of materials through a manufacturing company (see Figure 11.2).

An integrated approach

Although logistics is responsible for the whole flow of materials through an organization, in practice the responsibilities are often split into separate parts. Typically 'materials management' is responsible for moving materials into and through the organization, while 'physical distribution' is responsible for moving finished goods out to customers. Often, the whole function is divided into even more parts: planners might set the demand for raw materials, procurement organizes the purchase of these, transport looks after their delivery, materials-handling receives and moves goods into stores, production removes materials from stores and looks after stocks

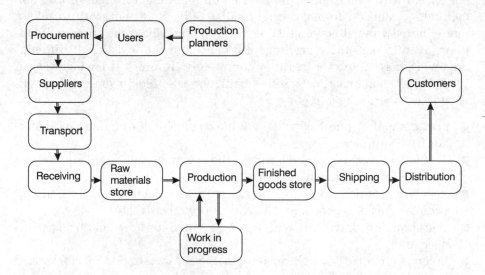

Figure 11.2 *Simplified material flow in a manufacturing company*

of work in progress, marketing controls the stocks of finished goods, and transport arranges delivery to customers.

Unfortunately, dividing logistics up like this creates artificial boundaries and can lead to serious inefficiencies. Different functions control a part of the materials flow, and they build their own administrations to deal with their parts, with no view of the bigger picture. This inevitably leads to duplication, wasted effort, inefficiency, poor communications and conflict. In extreme cases, there can be several systems for, say, controlling stocks, none of which are compatible or use the same standards. More importantly, the separate views of logistics have different objectives. Marketing, for example, might want high stocks of finished goods, a wide variety of products available close to customers, an extensive distribution network allowing products to be moved quickly to customers, and production to respond to orders from marketing. Production, on the other hand, might want little variation in products, to allow long production runs, high stocks of raw materials and work in progress, extensive production facilities with efficient flows of materials through operations, and marketing to respond to output from operations. Finance might take a completely different view, wanting low stocks everywhere, few facilities, and make-to-order operations.

The main problem with this fragmented approach to logistics is that each function tries to satisfy its own needs, often ignoring those of the whole organization. If purchasing wants to reduce its costs, it could buy large quantities, to reduce administration and receive quantity discounts. However, this brings an increase in the cost of stock-holding, which might more than offset the savings of procurement. In the same way, traffic could reduce the cost of inward transport by using local suppliers, but this might increase the purchase price paid by production.

The best way of overcoming such short-sighted decisions is to have one integrated logistics function in charge of all the movement of resources. This can take a broader view, balance the various objectives and achieve much better overall results.

Aims of integrated logistics

The aim of this integrated logistics function is to move resources into, through and out of an organization as effectively and efficiently as possible. In summary, logistics aims at getting 'the right quantity, of the right materials, to the right place, at the right time, from the right source, with the right quality, at the right price'. To be a little more specific, logistics aims to:

- design an effective and efficient supply chain;
- find the best locations and capacities for facilities;

- formulate strategies for guaranteeing the movement of all resources needed to satisfy customer demands;
- manage an efficient flow of materials into, through, and out of the process;
- ensure appropriate materials are procured from reliable suppliers;
- organize efficient handling of work in progress;
- find the best transport for reliable deliveries to customers;
- get low costs for storage and high stock turnover;
- maintain good relations with suppliers, customers and other interested parties;
- handle related information accurately and efficiently.

LOCATION

An integrated logistics function obviously involves decisions of many types. One of the most important relates to finding the best locations for facilities. Whenever an organization wants a new factory, warehouse, shop, office, or other facility, it has to make a decision about location. Clearly, this decision can affect the organization's performance for many years. If an electronics company opens a factory in the wrong location, it might find that the workforce is unskilled, productivity is low, the quality of products cannot be guaranteed, and all its costs are high. However, once a factory is opened, it is very difficult simply to close it down and move. In 1997, Siemens opened a factory in Newcastle, in the north of England, but, in 1998, with the economic decline in the Far East, they decided to close it. One of their first costs was to repay the £50 million they had received in government grants when deciding to open the factory.

> Facilities location aims at finding the best possible geographic location for an organization's operations.

There are many reasons why an organization may want to find a new location for its facilities. These include:
- the end of a lease on existing premises;
- a desire to expand into new geographical areas;
- changes in the location of customers or suppliers;
- significant changes in operations, which need a different type of location;
- upgrading of facilities, perhaps to introduce new technology;
- changes to the logistics system, such as changing from rail transport to road;
- changes in the transport network, such as the new bridge across the River Severn, or the Channel Tunnel.

Commercial estate agents often say (quoting a phrase attributed to Lord Sieff) that 'The three most important things for a successful business are location, location and location.' Certainly, the decisions about location are some of the most important an organization has to make. A nightclub, for example, is unlikely to do well in an area where most people are retired; a manufacturer with major markets in Western Europe would be unwise to locate outside the European Union; busy art galleries and museums are most successful at the centre of large cities.

Decisions about locations can determine the success or failure of an organization, and there are many examples of organizations that have located in the wrong place and gone out of business.

Management example – Canary Wharf

Olympia and York has built large office developments in many countries. In the late 1980s, it decided to build in the Isle of Dogs in East London. This was the biggest office development ever undertaken in Britain and among the biggest in Europe.

The Isle of Dogs was the old dock area of London, near the centre of the City; when the docks closed, a large, run-down area was left. This had obvious attractions for Olympia and York, particularly as the Government was offering incentives to promote development. Unfortunately, there were also drawbacks with the location and with the timing of the development.

Canary Wharf tried to attract companies that wanted office space in central London, but did not want the high costs of actually being within the main financial centre of the City. In practice, it proved difficult to attract companies away from the City to a more remote, less convenient site, which had poor transport and few facilities. Competing developers opened less prestigious – but more convenient – buildings nearer to the City, and the office vacancy rate at Canary Wharf rose to 17 per cent. This had an effect on average rents, which fell by 30 per cent. At the same time, Britain was in its worst recession since the 1930s, and most companies were struggling for survival rather than looking to expand into new premises.

By 1992, Olympia and York had serious financial difficulties, and its debts had risen to $20 billion. The company struggled through restructuring and changing ownership for several years before its future became more settled.

Alternatives to locating new facilities

Setting up new facilities is always expensive, and organizations often prefer to look at the alternatives. When, for example, a company decides to sell its goods in a new market, it can do this in five ways, which are listed below in order of increasing investment.

- Licensing/franchising: local companies make and distribute the company's products in return for a share of the profits.
- Exporting: the company makes the product in its existing facilities and sells it to a distributor in the new market.
- Local warehousing and sales: the company makes the product in its existing facilities, and sets up its own warehouses and salesforce to handle distribution in the new market.
- Local assembly/finishing: the company makes most of the product in existing facilities, but opens limited facilities in the new market to finish or assemble the final product.
- Full local production: the company opens complete facilities in the new market.

The advantages of local facilities include greater control over products, higher profits, avoidance of import tariffs and quotas, easier transportation, reduced costs and closer links with local customers. These benefits must be balanced against more complex and uncertain operations. The best alternative depends on many factors, such as the capital available, the risk the organization will accept, the target return on investment, existing operations, timescale, local knowledge, transport costs, tariffs, trade restrictions and the available workforce.

Choosing the geographic region for operations

If an organization decides to open new facilities, it has to make a hierarchy of decisions about the location. These start with a wide view, looking at the attractions of different countries or geographic regions. Then, it must consider the best areas within this country or region, then alternative towns and cities within the region, and, finally, different sites within the preferred town or city.

Starting at the top of this hierarchy, an organization has to decide the best region or country in which to work. Traditionally, it would open new facilities in a country where the long-term forecasts showed continuing demand for a product. More recently, organizations have opened facilities in new countries, not to be near their customers, but to take advantage of lower costs. Low wages in developing countries have encouraged many manufacturers to open factories in the Far East, South America and Eastern Europe, but low wage rates do not automatically mean low costs. Labour costs form a very small part of the total costs of many products; locations far away from major customers obviously lead to higher transport costs; and a more common problem is that low wages are often accompanied by very low productivity. Low wages alone do not guarantee low-cost operations.

Most organizations prefer to locate in an area that is near to their customers, has reliable suppliers and a good infrastructure, and a skilled workforce that gives high productivity and guaranteed quality, even if they will also have high labour costs. One of the earliest companies to notice this was the Tandy Corporation, which moved production of its latest computer to South Korea in 1980. However, rising shipping costs, the long sea voyage to the USA, the changing value of the dollar and a redesign of the product, to allow more automated production, made this location less attractive. In 1987, Tandy moved its production back to Fort Worth in Texas, and consequently reduced costs by 7.5 per cent.

The choice of the best country in which to locate operations can be very complicated, and involves many factors, including:

- costs: operating costs, wages, transport costs, energy, taxes, hidden costs;
- economic climate: currency exchange rates, exchange regulations, competition, availability of grants, inflation, rate of growth, productivity;
- social climate: language, culture, availability and skills of workforce, attitude towards organization, stability, reliability;
- political climate: political situation, stability, international relations, legal system;
- infrastructure: availability of transport, services;
- locations of other organizations: competitors, suppliers and customers;
- internal operations: locations of current operations, future expansion plans;
- organization: adopting international operations (running activities from a headquarters in the 'home' country) or multinational (with subsidiary organizations that are largely independent);
- operations: using the same operations around the world or adapting to the local environment.

Choosing the best site

Once a decision has been made about the country or geographical region, more detailed decisions need to be taken with regard to areas, towns, cities and individual sites. There are two distinct approaches to this:

Management example – McDonald's in Moscow

The world's largest McDonald's hamburger restaurant is in Moscow. This is operated jointly by McDonald's of Canada, which owns 49 per cent, and a local Russian company, which owns 51 per cent.

McDonald's has opened branches throughout the world, but this was one of the most difficult to set up. Negotiations started with the Soviet Union 20 years before the restaurant finally opened.

Inside the restaurant, everything follows the standard McDonald pattern, with the standard menu, colour scheme and decor, staff training, and levels of cleanliness and cooking. However, this could only be achieved with considerable effort, and only when conditions in Russia changed. As well as the obvious political problems, there were significant practical problems. Beef in Moscow is not readily available and the quality is poor. McDonald's had to import breeding cattle and start a beef farm in order to supply the restaurant. Potatoes are plentiful, but they are the wrong type to make McDonald's fries, so seed potatoes were imported and grown. Russian cheese was not suitable for cheeseburgers, so a dairy plant was opened to make processed cheese.

Although the restaurant is very popular, the initial set-up cost was so high that the restaurant does not expect to make a profit in the foreseeable future.

- infinite set approach – which uses geometric arguments to show where the best site would be if there were no restrictions on availability;
- feasible set approach – which compares the feasible sites that are actually available and chooses the best.

Infinite set approaches

Infinite set models look at the geographic layout of customers and suppliers, and find the location that minimizes some measure of performance. The best location is usually near the centre of potential demands and supplies, and a simple calculation finds the 'centre of gravity' of demand. This centre of gravity can give a reasonably good location, but it is only a starting point, as there may be no site available anywhere near the centre of gravity, or, if a site is available, it may be too expensive, it might be a long way from roads and services, it might be in an area with no workforce, or even in a river. This problem is common to all such methods, and means that infinite set approaches are most useful for cutting down the area of search for a location. Then a feasible set approach can be used to compare available locations within this smaller area.

Feasible set approach

The feasible set approach compares alternative sites. The two most common ways of doing this are to use a costs model or a scoring model.

The costing model method simply estimates the total costs of operating in each site. A simple view could concentrate on:

- operating cost – the total cost of running the facility;
- inward transport cost – the cost of moving goods and services into the facility from suppliers;
- outward transport cost – the cost of moving finished goods and services out to customers.

There are, of course, many variations on these costing models, and many costs could be included – the best amount of detail depends on the circumstances.

The simple model mentioned emphasizes the cost of logistics, and assumes that most other costs are fixed. Ideally, this would suggest a location that is near to both suppliers and customers. Often, however, the suppliers are some distance away from the customers and a compromise location is needed. If this location is near to the suppliers, it will have low costs for inward transport, but high costs for outward transport; if it is near to the customers, it will have low costs for outward transport, but high costs for inward transport (as shown in Figure 11.3).

An obvious problem with this approach is that actual costs are not known in advance. An organization cannot know how much outward transport will cost when the customers and their demands are not known before opening. Even if the costs are known, they depend on the accounting conventions used, and will change over time. These costing models give useful comparisons, but they do not show the real costs. Perhaps more importantly, they do not take into account the wide range of factors that cannot be costed.

A scoring model may be a more appropriate alternative in other circumstances, particularly when certain factors that are important for location decisions cannot be quantified. It is difficult, for example, to put a cost on the attractive lifestyle offered by a location, although this would certainly benefit employees, reduce staff turnover and assist in recruiting. Other factors may be important, but are difficult to quantify. For country and region, these may include the following:

- availability and skills of workforce;
- climate;
- local and national government policies;

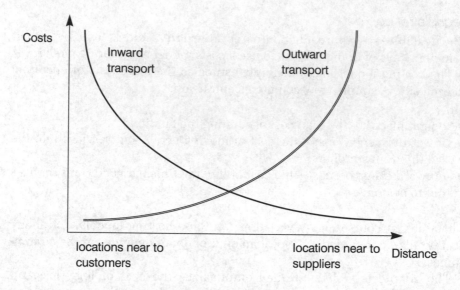

Figure 11.3 *Transport costs and facility location*

- availability of development grants;
- attractiveness of locations;
- environment and quality of life, including health, education, welfare and culture;
- reliability of local suppliers and services;
- infrastructure, particularly transport and communications;
- economic and political stability.

Factors that are difficult to quantify, which relate to the city or to the site, may include the following:

- closeness of customers, suppliers and services;
- location of competitors;
- location of retail shops and other attractions;
- convenience for roads and public transport;
- ease of access, visibility and convenience of parking;
- population density and socio-economic characteristics;
- labour relations and community attitude;
- local restrictions on operations;
- potential for expansion.

Using a scoring model is a good way of considering such non-quantifiable factors. The procedure for this is as follows:

1. decide the relevant factors in a decision;
2. give each factor a maximum possible score that shows its importance;
3. consider each location in turn and give an actual score for each factor;
4. add the total score for each location and find the highest;
5. discuss the result and make a final decision.

Management example – Bowen Electronics

When Jim Bowen looked at locations for a new electronics warehouse, he wanted it to be in Western Canada, relatively close to his existing operations, but allowing expansion into new areas. He quickly identified sites near to four cities, and made a tentative list of important factors, their relative weights, and scores for each site:

Factor	Maximum	A	B	C	D
Climate	10	8	6	9	7
Infrastructure	20	12	16	15	8
Accessibility	10	6	8	7	9
Construction cost	5	3	1	4	2
Community attitude	10	6	8	7	4
Government views	5	2	2	3	4
Closeness to suppliers	15	10	10	13	13
Closeness to customers	20	12	10	15	17
Availability of workers	5	1	2	4	5
Totals	100	60	63	77	69

This was obviously a quick analysis, and Bowen added many more factors before he thought about his decision in earnest. None the less, this simple approach suggested that location C was worth serious attention, and this is where Bowen eventually built his warehouse.

There are many models and methods that can help with location decisions. One useful general approach does the following:

- uses an infinite set approach to find a reasonable location for facilities;
- searches near this location to find a set of reasonable, available locations;
- uses a feasible set approach to compare these alternatives;
- adds costs and other information to a scoring model;
- discusses all available information and comes to a final decision.

Management example – Hamburg Double Glazed Windows

Hamburg Double Glazed Windows (HDGW) is one of Europe's largest manufacturers of UPVC windows. It ran three plants around Hamburg: a plastics works that made the UPVC and exuded contours for window frames, a glassworks, and an assembly works for making the complete windows. The first two of these plants had automated processes that needed little manual work. The third plant – where the windows were actually assembled – had little automation and was labour-intensive.

In 1995, the assembly works had serious labour problems, and there was a long strike by workers. After the strike was settled, the average wage rate in the plant was nearly twice the industrial average for Germany. HDGW now had high costs, was much less competitive, and lost a lot of market share to its rivals. In an effort to reduce costs, HDGW decided to move its assembly plant to an area just outside Barcelona in Spain. The two main reasons for choosing this site were: the Spanish Government and European Union gave generous incentives and that Barcelona could provide cheap, unskilled labour.

In the longer term, HDGW thought that it would save 10 million Deutschmarks a year by this move. They decided to move all their assembly equipment from Hamburg to Barcelona, and estimated that this would take 6 months to complete, with another 6 months to sort out any production problems. The company lost 64 of its 68 managers when they accepted a redundancy package rather than move, and almost all their experienced salaried employees left. All the hourly paid workers in the Hamburg works were laid off.

HDGW hired 200 people in Barcelona with wages at about one-quarter of the German equivalent. Unfortunately, these recruits spoke only Spanish, while the company's instructions and procedure manuals were all in German, and the staff in Hamburg spoke almost no Spanish. The resulting language barrier – together with increasingly obvious cultural differences – created serious problems with supervision, training, efficiency, motivation and productivity. Not surprisingly, costs rose more than expected.

There were also technical problems. Some of the assembly machines were damaged in the move, and the last phase of transfer from Hamburg to Barcelona was stopped, to avoid the risk of more damage. Then, increasing fuel prices raised the cost of moving materials from the two plants in Hamburg to the assembly works in Barcelona, as well as the cost of shipping finished windows back to the main markets in Northern Europe.

Three years after the start of the relocation project, there is still no end in sight to the company's problems. Costs have turned out to be considerably higher than anticipated and the company's market share is still falling.

PROCUREMENT

Procurement is the first real step in the flow of resources through an organization, and forms an important link between suppliers and operations. In general, purchasing refers to the actual buying of materials, while procurement has a broader meaning and can include purchasing, contracting, expediting, materials handling, transport, warehousing and receiving goods from suppliers.

■ Procurement describes the range of activities that are responsible for acquiring the resources needed by an organization.
■ Its aim is to ensure that all the resources needed are available at the right time, and the supply is as effective and efficient as possible.

If a process does not have the resources it needs, it cannot work – and there might be interrupted operations, unmet customer demand, high costs, delayed deliveries, and reduced productivity. Procurement makes sure that resources are available when they are needed. Some of its more specific objectives are to:

■ work closely with user department and understands their needs;
■ buy the resources needed by operations;
■ make sure these have reliably high quality;
■ makes sure they arrive at the right time;
■ expedite deliveries when necessary;
■ find reliable suppliers, work closely with them and develop good relations;
■ negotiate low prices from suppliers;
■ keep informed about price increases, scarcities, and so on;
■ keep inventory levels low, by buying standard materials, and so on.

To achieve these aims, procurement usually works with a purchase cycle, which typically includes the following steps.

■ User department – the person needing the goods or services makes a request; this is checked against budgets and plans; a purchase request is sent to procurement.

- Then, procurement – analyses the purchase request; verifies and checks the details; checks current stocks, alternative products, planned purchases, etc; makes a shortlist of possible suppliers; sends a request for quotations to this shortlist.
- Then, the suppliers – examine the request for quotations; see how they could best satisfy the order; send offers back to the organization, with prices, specifications, conditions and delivery.
- Then, procurement: compares quotations and chooses the best supplier; discusses and finalizes details with the chosen supplier; sends a purchase order to the chosen supplier.
- Then, the chosen supplier – processes the purchase order; makes or prepares the order; ships goods, prepares services and sends an invoice.
- Then, procurement does any necessary follow-up or expediting; receiving inspects and accepts goods and updates files; warehousing stores goods and updates inventory records; finance arranges payment of the invoice; users withdraw goods when they are needed.

There are, of course, many variations on this general pattern. Inexpensive items do not need to go through such a complex procedure, while very expensive items need much more care. One important point, though, is that the lowest price does not necessarily represent the best buy. As with TQM, a product must be judged by a whole range of factors, and only one of these is cost. Most organizations are willing to pay more than the minimum for products that are always reliable and delivered on time.

With an understanding of the function of procurement, it is possible to see why it is so important. It forms the main link between an organization and its suppliers, and is essential for any process. The operations will only run smoothly if procurement is carried out effectively, and any faults will appear as poor-quality materials, late deliveries, wrong quantities, interrupted operations, high costs, and poor customer service. Another important point is that a typical organization spends 60 per cent of its income on purchases, so procurement is responsible for the majority of the expenditure. This gives considerable potential for savings and increased profits. If an organization has a profit margin of 10 per cent, a 1 per cent reduction in the cost of purchased goods will increase profits by 6 per cent. This is demonstrated by seeing what happens when the organization sells £100 of products.

Original		Changed	
Sales £100		£100	
Cost of purchases	£60	£59.40	– reduced by 1 per cent
Other costs	£30	£30	
Profit £10		£10.60	– increased by 6 per cent

The role of procurement has changed significantly in recent years. It used to be little more than a clerical job, buying materials as they were requested. Now, its importance is more widely recognized and it has become a profession with managers expected to take an active part in planning. General Motors spends over $50 billion a year in purchasing materials, so it is not surprising that very senior managers are involved.

Management example – accounts payable at Ford

In 1988 Ford of America was looking for increased productivity in their accounts payable department. This employed 500 people, who worked a standard accounting system, in which:

- the purchase department sent a purchase order to the vendor and a copy to accounts payable;
- the vendor shipped the goods ordered;
- when the goods arrived at Ford, a clerk at the receiving dock checked them, completed a form describing the goods and sent it to accounts payable;
- the vendor sent an invoice to accounts payable;
- accounts payable now had three descriptions of the goods – from the purchase order, receipt form and invoice. If these matched, the invoice was paid, but in a few cases there were discrepancies, which could take weeks to trace and clear up.

Ford thought that they could save perhaps 25 per cent of staffing costs by redesigning the system. They looked at Mazda, which was running its accounts payable using far fewer staff than Ford were. In the end, Ford re-engineered the system, so that:

- the purchase department sends a purchase order to the vendor, and enters details on a database;
- the vendor ships the goods ordered;
- when the goods arrive at Ford, a clerk at the receiving dock checks the database to see if they correspond to an outstanding order. If they do, the clerk updates the database to show that the goods have arrived, and the computer automatically sends a cheque to the supplier. If there are discrepancies, the clerk refuses to accept the delivery and sends it back to the supplier.

Returning goods seems drastic, but suppliers rarely make more than one mistake, and they are pleased that the approach of 'we pay when we receive the invoice' has changed to 'we pay when we receive the goods'. The new system is operated by 125 people, giving a 400 per cent increase in productivity.

PHYSICAL DISTRIBUTION

Procurement moves resources into an organization, and forms the main link between a process and its suppliers. At the other end of the operations, physical distribution moves finished goods out from the organization, and forms an important link between a process and the customers. This means that physical distribution forms the final link in a supply cycle, as shown in Figure 11.4.

A typical distribution system moves products from production departments to warehouses, where they are stored until they are sent to customers. There can be several levels of regional and local warehouses between production and the customer (see Figure 11.5). This kind of distribution system has developed to deal with operations that are some distance away from customers. Manufacturers, for example, aim for economies of scale by concentrating production in a few large facilities, while retail shops provide small, local services that are near to customers. The distribution system is needed to connect these two. There are several advantages of a system based on wholesalers and intermediaries:

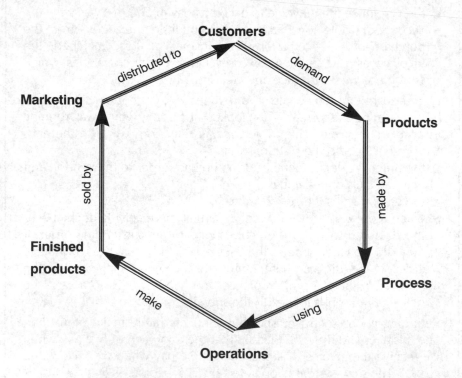

Figure 11.4 *Distribution in a supply chain*

- production can achieve economies of scale by concentrating operations in central locations;
- production facilities need not keep large stocks of finished goods;
- wholesalers keep stocks from many suppliers, allowing retailers a choice of goods;
- wholesalers are near to retailers and have short lead times;
- wholesalers can place large orders and reduce unit prices;
- retailers can carry less stock as wholesalers offer reliable delivery times;
- distribution costs are reduced by moving large orders from production facilities to wholesalers, rather than moving small orders directly to retailers or customers.

This kind of distribution system is easily imagined for manufacturers, but it is also used by services. Airlines, for example, have major hub airports with feeder services to regional airports, and then short hauls to local airports; banks collect all cheques in central clearing houses before sending them back to branches and customers; blood banks have regional centres that act as wholesalers.

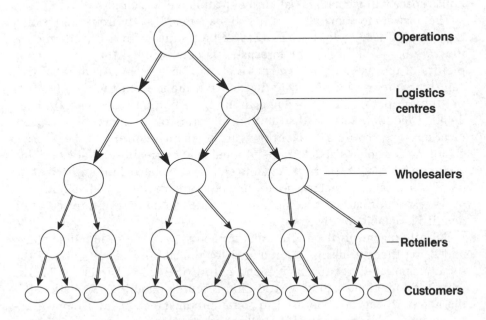

Figure 11.5 *A typical distribution system*

Decisions for physical distribution

Physical distribution involves decisions that range from the long-term strategic through to the short-term operational. Perhaps the fundamental decisions concern the shape of the distribution system: How many warehouses should there be? How big will each one be? Where will they be located?

Alongside these decisions is the choice of mode of transport. Most goods in the UK travel by road, so it is important for all facilities to have easy access to the road network. However, there is increasing pressure for bulky materials to use rail, or even water and pipeline. The other type of transport is air, which is only cheap enough for small loads of expensive materials. The best mode of transport obviously depends on the type of goods to be moved, distances, weights, value and a whole range of other things. Realistically, the majority of goods will continue to be distributed by road for the foreseeable future, and this effectively limits the choices for design of a distribution system.

When the strategic decisions have been made, and the distribution system has been designed, it is time for questions to be asked relating to the lower-level decisions: How much will we move to customers? How many vehicles will we need? What routes will they take? How much warehouse space will we use? What kind of people will we employ?

The answers to some of these questions come directly from the production plans. These show how much will be produced in a period, and, as they are based on actual, or forecast, customer orders, they give a good picture of the types of movements that will be needed. An organization can, therefore, design its basic distribution plans from the details of its production plan. If it adds some input from marketing, it can find the detailed requirements for distribution, in terms of products to be moved, product mix, volumes reaching warehouses, amounts to be stored, customer locations, size and variety of customer demands, details of deliveries and timing. These requirements can be translated into a distribution plan, which sets the materials-handling equipment, transport fleet, number of drivers, information systems, and so on. Eventually, this can lead to a detailed timetable for distribution.

This approach, of finding the requirements from the production plans, and using them to design a timetable for distribution, is essentially the same as materials requirement planning or MRP (see Chapter 8). This is why it is sometimes called 'distribution resource planning'. As with MRP, the approach can only be used in some circumstances, and a more traditional approach to planning is usually needed.

IMPORTANCE OF LOGISTICS

Although it is easier to imagine distribution for manufacturers or retailers, it is really needed in every kind of organization. Every organization uses operations to make a product, and every organization needs a distribution system to pass these products on to customers. In the same way that efficient operations are needed to make the products, efficient distribution is needed to make sure that they reach the customers. In the past, distribution was often under-valued; it was considered to be an essential service, the cost of which was added to other overheads. However, in recent years, its importance has been recognized, and it is an area in which significant savings can be made. This new view can be summarized by saying that distribution is important because it:

- is essential;
- is expensive;
- directly affects profitability;
- provides the main link between an organization and its customers;
- affects lead time and service levels;
- can give a competitive advantage;
- gives public exposure with trucks and other facilities;
- can be risky, with safety considerations;
- determines the best size and location of facilities;
- may prohibit some operations – such as moving excessive loads;
- can encourage the development of other organizations.

CHAPTER REVIEW

- Logistics is responsible for the flow of materials from suppliers, through operations and on to final customers. It aims to give a smooth flow of materials through the supply chain.
- Logistics interacts with every other function in an organization and consists of a number of related jobs, including procurement, materials management, warehousing, transport, distribution, forecasting and inventory control.
- Although logistics is often spread over different functions within an organization, there are considerable benefits in having a single integrated logistics function to organize the movement of all materials.
- A key element of logistics is to find the best location for activities. These are strategic decisions, with consequences felt over the long

term. Location decisions start by looking for the best region or country, then move through decisions about the best area, town and, eventually, specific site.
- Many models can help with location decisions. These take two distinct approaches, either using geometric arguments to suggest where the best location would be in principle, or comparing a limited number of feasible locations to find the best.
- Procurement makes sure that an organization has the resources it needs for its operations. This is the major link between operations and suppliers. It is responsible for the majority of the costs of many processes.
- At the other end of the supply chain is physical distribution, which is concerned with moving finished products from operations out to final customers. This is responsible for the design of the overall distribution system, and then for making sure that it works efficiently.

FURTHER READING

Bailey, P and Farmer, D (1994) *Purchasing Principles and Management* (7th edition), Pitman Publishing, London

Chadwick, T and Rajagopal, S (1995) *Strategic Supply Chain Management*, Butterworth-Heinemann, London

Coyle, J J, Bardi, E J, and Langley, C J (1996) *The Management of Business Logistics* (6th edition), West, St Paul, Mn

Stock, J R and Lambert, D M (1987) *Strategic Logistics Management* (2nd edition) Richard D. Irwin, Homewood, Il

Index

Page reference in *italics* indicate figures or tables